THE TOUCH OF LOVE

An Intimate Journey with a Surrogate Partner

Cheryl King

ISBN: 0615801889
ISBN 13: 9780615801889
Library of Congress Control Number: 2014916498
Sunleaf Press, San Pablo, CA

TESTIMONIALS

..”Once I had worked with Cheryl King, I did some dating until I found my present wife. When I told her that I hadn't had a lot of relationships, she wouldn't believe me and said I must have had sex with a lot of women. Cheryl was a wonderful partner and teacher and I will always be grateful for her help. It changed my life.”   P.D.

..”Cheryl was kind, honest, patient, intuitive and had a great sense of humor, which really put me at ease. I can truthfully say that my life now would not have been possible, if it wasn't for her. I went to her as an inexperienced, middle-aged virgin and now I'm dating and very hopeful about my future.” J.L.

…*"The therapist that I had been seeing for some years suggested that I see a sex surrogate when I developed Peyronies disease. I had become embarrassed and insecure about my ability to have sex and consequently had stopped seeing anyone. He found Cheryl King's name and she agreed to see me. She was great! She helped me to be comfortable with my body and we found ways that I could still be sexual, even with my problem and I will always be grateful to her for that and for her empathy and compassion."* K.A.

"…I was a socially clueless virgin male nearing my 30s. What I needed more than anything else was a surrogate friend to teach me how to relate and carry on a proper conversation and date other people. Cheryl was that compassionate, caring person and teacher." T.N.

"…Cheryl is an extraordinarily gifted surrogate partner therapist. Her greatest strength is in being able to recognize her client's unique needs and sensitivities and to create a safe environment where they can work through their deepest fears about intimacy and sex. I have never worked with a more caring or effective therapist." R.P.

"….A gifted healer of the heart, mind, body and soul, Cheryl has the ability to sense others on many different levels. She is a great listener, and responds with warmth, compassion, and a refreshing playfulness. Deeply empathic, Cheryl creates a place of safety that helps her clients to express their wants and

desires, their conflicts and fears. From there, she gently guides them from the places they may feel stuck into those parts of themselves that have been longing to live and find expression. Working with Cheryl can change your life in ways you have hoped and longed for.

John Porterfield   MFT

ACKNOWLEDGEMENTS

I want to express my deepest gratitude to my husband Tom, for lovingly and generously supporting me in my work and for constantly encouraging me to complete this book.

I would also like to thank Suzanne Schellenberg for her editing skills, design creativity, helpful and comforting knowledge of the mysteries of Word and for putting up with my indecision.

A special thanks to Vicki Dotterer for seeing something in me and giving me the gift of Leslie Keenan's class "So You think You Have a Book In You," without which, this book would never have happened. And to Leslie and her Thursday writing group, my deep appreciation for listening, gently and helpfully critiquing and being so open to and appreciative of the subject matter.

To the members of our couples group: Annette and George Salvaggio and Cathie and Peter Eliaser, and Gailya Magdalena, Michelle Groleau, Martha Daetwyler, Louie Sheridan and Caroline McKinnon of my women's group, my sincere appreciation for your encouragement over the endless years it has taken me to complete this book.

For the Palm Springs Gang; John Glasser, John Porterfield, Joel Matthews and my dear friend Rae Baird, a big hug of gratitude for your support and patience with me.

And last, but definitely not least, a huge, sweet thank you to Vena Blanchard of IPSA who trained me, has been my friend and has been ever supportive of my work and me.

INTRODUCTION

This is a book about the power of sexuality and love for healing, and it is the story of one sexual surrogate partner's process of surrogate therapy. At the most basic level, SPT can change the way one moves about in the world and infuse one's every day life with the awareness of the possibilities for a fully lived life and the potential for excitement, comfort, pleasure and love. For some, just to feel normal is a great healing.

Surrogate therapy offers this gift: To feel like a fully functional human being and a person capable of finding, creating and sustaining a loving relationship. Those deprived of these things often feel like an outsider, separate from the rest of humanity by their secret feeling of brokenness, the feeling that there is something wrong with them that can't be fixed. Loneliness and isolation, however, can be great drivers to the destination of wholeness.

It takes courage to embark on a course of change no matter how desperately one longs for it, but surrogate therapy offers hope and healing. It is also reciprocal, as the process of introspection and challenging our own old patterns offers healing for the surrogate partner as well.

I have used a client James, who is actually my representation of a typical mid life virgin, to demonstrate the model of surrogate therapy and the steps involved in the process. To be expedient I have, for the most part, told the story as though each step followed consecutively, however in actuality, it is often necessary to linger at one step or another, or even take a step backward. This would depend on the client's area of difficulty and their ability to sustain a sense of comfort and safety.

Also, this is my story, based on my personality and the way I work. Each surrogate has her own approach and healing gifts that she or he offers, but I believe that the premise and the basic model generally remain the same among us.

I have two hopes for this book: One is that it will encourage women and men who feel they have a calling

or a talent for this work, to consider it and seek training. Whether straight, gay, or bi-sexual, the need for
compassionate, loving and open healers is great and
there are too few of us. Secondly and more importantly, that it will serve as hope for healing, as an awareness
of sensual potential, and especially for those who feel
they have no choice in living their life fully, with love
and pleasure, to know that there is compassionate help
waiting out there.

CHAPTER 1
THE POWER AND POTENTIAL OF SENSUALITY AND SEXUALITY

When I think of my own sexual experiences, I feel them as emotional and energetic, rather than actually physical. Memories of the physical acts of intercourse that I've had over my life tend to run and blur together, like the colors of oil on water.

My attachment to any sexual experience is to the heightened awareness of each moment, to the scent of

1

my own breath on another's skin and the sound of our breath together, to the intense feelings of connection and the flow of my own sensual personalities coming forward and interacting with my partner. It is the pleasure of discovery, the amazement that I feel watching my partner's pleasure and the luscious dreaminess of the touch that explores my curves and swells and the hidden and greedy secret parts of me.

It is the beauty of an arched foot that breaks my heart in the moment or the mouth that bites voraciously at the back of my neck. It is feeling vulnerable, and powerful in that vulnerability. It is the opening, consciously letting my lover into me, into my body and into my heart. Giving up my soul to the moment, to allow it to feel what it is to be in body, connected to another soul. It is the beauty, as well as the danger or rawness of words, spoken, murmured or sworn. It is myself unleashed, biting, sucking, licking, controlling, taking my own pleasure. It is eyes wide with surprise, eyes spilling tears, unable to contain the largeness of emotion. It is laughter, pain, compassion, rage, joy, tenderness, sorrow, childishness, wisdom, strength and fragility. It is darkness and light. It is a crossing over to another land and returning with more of my self.

All this is the power and potential of sexuality. Of course, not every sexual experience I've had has contained the depth I've shared here, but this is what I always seek, even in small moments, and I am always rewarded.

My own personal sex life is very different from my work as a surrogate partner, but some of the basics of the work are things that have come very naturally to me, like the foundation of surrogate therapy, sensate focus touch. Going through the exercises in sensate touch is like home to me. Touching my partner in ways that bring me pleasure, that let me explore and play with their body, is something that I have always done. I believe in touch. It is to me the most immediate form of communication, sensing on energetic levels. It can put someone at ease or on guard instantly. It can communicate neediness or passion, caring or lack of presence.

Sensate focus is touching another for one's own pleasure without goals. In the beginning it's done one active partner at a time, paying attention to one's own sensation, focusing on the details and taking pleasure in the temperature of the skin, the different textures, the hidden curve of the inside elbow or back of the knee. For me, it could include sliding across the smoothness of the shoulder and down the long muscles of the back, gliding, and eventually using my whole body to dance on my partner. It is not massage and while it can be only the fingertips touching the body at times, for me it is experiencing the palm of my hand or the inside of my forearm on a body that gives me the most sensation. When I add that attention to my whole body, it becomes a delightful dance of pleasure.

I've had people ask me sometimes, "But what about the other person, the one who's being touched, if the active one is taking their own pleasure?"

I usually reply, "Well, the receiving partner simply relaxes and receives, paying attention to their own sensations, and I can assure you that when you're receiving that much attention and connectedness you are going to have pleasure too."

Working with a client, starts from the ground up, beginning with lots of breath exercises for relaxation. Some clients have great anxiety around touching and being touched, so the work goes slowly, beginning with hands and arms only, centering the client and bringing them back, again and again, out of the mind that judges, critiques and watches, into the sensate self, into what is being felt, rather than thought. Some clients are so ready for change, ready to step into their sexual self, even if tentatively, that they take to the sensate touch with great pleasure.

For most people, it is the first time that they have touched or have been touched in this way and it's an eye opener to the possibilities for pleasure. It is also a place to come back to when anxiety tries to take over, or when too much focus on a partner as in, "Does she like this," "Am I doing it right for her," or "She's not moving!" takes one out of one's own body and into the land of "uh, oh, I'm losing it," meaning their arousal.

Once I feel that the client is well grounded in the experience of sensate focus, we begin to move on to using it on faces and then to the rest of the body. It's a whole process over many sessions before we arrive at the "is intercourse necessary with this client" part. It is the beginning point and is the avenue to learning to receive pleasure and eventually to give pleasure as well.

CHAPTER 2

JAMES FIRST SESSION

N ow let me take you on a healing journey with my representational client James and myself. I get my referrals from therapists or from IPSA, the International Professional Surrogates Association (Yes, indeed there is an association, based in Los Angeles that trains and certifies surrogate partners). In an effort to show the relationship aspect of this therapy, I have described my own experience as a surrogate.

One day I received a call from one of my favorite therapists telling me that he had a new client for me, a 44 year-old man, with erectile difficulties that had prevented him from beginning relationships. His experience had been limited to a couple of failed experiences in his early twenties. James felt he had a low sex drive and admitted to strong feelings of anxiety around the idea of sexuality. He was an educated professional and had work acquaintances, but had never cultivated any real friendships. His upbringing was in an extremely religious household, where sexuality was never mentioned and displays of affection were rare. It was clear to Dr. Johnston, that James had lacked appropriate emotional models with which to develop a sexual and relational self.

James said that he had now come to a time in his life when he wanted to change and dreamed of a possible family some day, but his two previous sexual experiences and the embarrassment and humiliation he felt over not being able to perform, caused him to be afraid that any interaction with women would eventually lead to the same.

Dr. Johnston had met with James for several months and felt he would greatly benefit from working with a professional surrogate in overcoming the anxiety and self-imposed isolation he'd experienced in his emotional and sexual life. He felt that by using surrogacy to provide James with a successful intimate experience, he would be able to overcome his fears and finally be able to achieve the emotional and physical closeness he hoped for.

I assured him that I felt that I certainly could help alleviate James' anxiety and build his confidence and agreed to take the case and my colleague assured me that he would give my contact information to James.

Normally we would have a three way meeting, the therapist the client and I, just for the client and I to get acquainted, but schedules were not compatible this time, so it was agreed that I would simply see the client at my home and make my report to Dr. Johnston. I was comfortable with that agreement as the two of them had been seeing each other for some time and I trusted Dr. Johnston's judgment.

A few days later James called and we scheduled an appointment for a two-hour intake session. I told him that we would get to know each other for the first hour and if we were comfortable with each other and felt we could work together, then we would agree to continue on into the second hour and the first of the least stressful exercises, sensate caresses on hands and arms.

I see my clients in my home, where I am comfortable and surrounded by beautiful things and a warm, and safe environment. An office would be fine with me, but I've never been able to find a type of place that I felt supported the intimacy of the work. People walking up and down the hall outside, or doors opening and closing, or the murmur of muffled voices could be anxiety provoking or, at the least, distracting.

The following week as the time of the appointment approached, I put on my makeup, using all my little tricks, to minimize the crow's feet around my eyes, and the wrinkles under them and to hide the variations in color in my skin. I applied my creams and concealers, my shadows, blushes and lipsticks and stood back to examine my artwork.

Ultimately, sensuality works it's magic between myself and a client and age and appearance don't matter, but clients often come into therapy with a pre-approved package in mind of what a surrogate should look like and occasionally, when I don't fit that notion of beauty or allure, they don't stay. Happily, it doesn't happen often. Most of the time if the person is comfortable with me, and will stay, the magic of the work takes over.

But at that moment, I was nervous and feeling a little vulnerable myself, as I was a good deal older than the man coming to my door. I've had younger clients than him, successfully, but that first meeting is always uncertain. What is always interesting to me, is that when the doorbell rings and I open the door, something older and wiser and more confident in me steps forth and I'm through the unknown and into the moment, present with what is and what is to be.

It happened again, when James rang the bell. There was a moment of wondering what he would look like and then I opened the door and there he was. A fairly average looking guy, brown eyes, brown hair touched with a little gray, a slightly receding hairline, and a pleasant, if terrified face. He was about 6 feet, and his black polo shirt outside of his khaki's hid a bit of a belly. He was dressed casually, carefully, and looked as though he took some care of himself. I invited him in and shook his hand and he introduced himself.

"Hi, Cheryl? I'm James."

"Yes, hi James. Come in," I responded, smiling.

I showed him in and introduced him to my couch, furnished him with a glass of water, for the inevitable dry throat, and we sat down together, he on the edge of the couch and myself, lightly ensconced against a cushion. My first task was to get him to relax, so I asked him to take a few deep breaths, sit back and make himself comfortable, which he did his best to do, and we began to talk. We were into our first session.

"So, did you have any trouble finding the place?" I asked, trying to give him time to settle himself, look around, look at me, or more the case, not look at me.

"No, your directions were easy to follow," he said "and it didn't take as long as I thought, so I stopped at the mall below and got a cup of coffee. I wasn't sure I was going to get here, but I did." I knew he didn't simply mean finding his way to my address.

"I'm glad you did, because, whatever you're experiencing, it must have been important for you to decide to look into this therapy. How are you feeling? Nervous, I imagine?"

James nodded and looked a little relieved to be acknowledging his anxiety.

"Well, I'm a little nervous myself," I said, "but we'll take some time today to get to know each other and see if we're comfortable enough to work together. Dr. Johnston has given me his report about your work with him, but I prefer to get the information straight from you, if that's okay?"

He nodded with a little shrug that said it was no big deal to relate it all again.

"Okay. Well, why don't you tell me what's brought you here, to sit on my couch."

He paused, preparing himself to tell his story. "Well, I haven't dated very much and I don't have much experience with women." He hesitated again, his hands tight on his thighs. "I tried to have sex a couple of times a long time ago, but it wasn't working." He looked off to one side as he caught the corner of his lip between his teeth. "I guess I just got scared to try it again." The next sentence came out in a rush, his embarrassment visible in his hunched shoulders.

"Time just kept going by and I started feeling like women would think I was gay, or a freak, because I wouldn't be able to do it. It was just easier to not go out with them. I suppose some people I work with do think I'm gay, because I never have dates, but I'm sure I'm not." His pause spoke volumes. "I just don't know what to do. Do you ever get people in here like me that turn out to be gay? I used to be attracted to women, but anymore I don't feel much. Could I be gay and not know it?" He turned to look at me squarely for the first time, his anxiety clear in the fine misting of sweat on his upper lip.

This is a question that I'm asked occasionally by inexperienced clients and I see it as an expression of their lack of awareness of their own sexuality. They simply don't see themselves as a sexual being and don't have any relationship to themselves or even others, in that way.

Occasionally however, a client has same sex attraction and is denying it, trying to fit in with what family or society or they themselves think they should be. In that case my work would be to help them accept and appreciate their true feelings.

"Have you ever felt an attraction to men?" I asked quietly, without judgment, simply wanting to know what level of thought he might have given the idea.

"No, I don't really think so…." he hesitated. "I can tell when a guy is good looking, but I don't feel attracted, you know, *that* way. But then, I don't with women anymore either. I don't let myself think about it much."

I shifted slightly and made myself more comfortable, relaxing into the sofa cushions, conveying, I imagined, my lack of concern over his sexual orientation.

"Well, it sounds to me like things have just happened to keep you from discovering your sexuality. I don't think we need to even worry about who you might be attracted to at this stage James. I think as we go along, making progress and you start experiencing a feeling of sexuality, you'll have a better idea about yourself and who you really find attractive." I smiled reassuringly.

"But, right now I'd like to hear more about your life, your family maybe. Perhaps you can tell me some about how things were for you growing up?"

James finally sat back and began to relax a bit. I guessed he realized that I wasn't going to jump on him right now.

"Yeah, I think we were a pretty average family, no abuse or weirdness or anything like that. There's four of us kids, one brother and sister older than me and one younger brother."

Many clients perceive their family as pretty average in the beginning, but as time goes by we might begin to see the family dynamics more clearly and where problems really began.

"My dad worked, traveled some and my mom stayed home and both of them were busy in the church. I was an altar boy at one point, which I hated, but they really wanted me to be one, especially my mom, so I stuck it out for a couple of years."

James shrugged, "All of us kids went on to college and got good jobs and that's about it. My brothers and sister are all married and have kids and I'm just Uncle Jamie. They never ask me why I'm not dating or married, but my sister keeps trying to fix me up with her friends now and then and I have to figure out how to get out of it, so who knows what she thinks about me!" His expression was rueful.

"It's really uncomfortable, but, if I didn't have this problem, I would like to meet someone. I'm kind of tired of being alone, you know?" He tilted his head to look at me sideways, his raised eyebrows asking for understanding.

I hoped that my eyes and face reflected that I understood his feeling. "Yeah, I'm sure you must feel that way. How are you feeling now, talking about all this?" I questioned, seeing for myself that his breathing was easier and that he was more relaxed, although his fingers were now tapping busily on his thighs. He faced straight ahead and turned his head as he spoke to me.

"Better," he responded, "I'm more comfortable."

"Good, that's what we want. I would like to ask you, do you think you could turn your body a bit, so that we can speak face to face a little better?"

He agreed and as he hitched one hip deeper into the sofa to make the shift to half-turn toward me, I explained that this is the first of the lessons in body language, that turning your body to whomever you're with indicates an openness and an interest. It was something he would need to know as he began dating. It also shows a certain confidence and a respect for the other.

We talked awhile longer about his life in general, his interests, his work, and his home. He had done fairly well for himself financially and owned his own condo, but told me that he didn't feel he'd done much with it and wouldn't be comfortable inviting anyone there. We'd get into that at a later date, maybe with my going over and checking it out.

I asked James if he could tell me about his sexual experiences. "Well, I didn't really date in high school, although I did go to a couple of dances with a girl. I was just too nervous around girls. I was always afraid I'd do something stupid and they'd think I was a jerk, so I just avoided them mostly. I didn't have too many guy friends either, though. I never felt comfortable having kids over to my house, I don't know why." He paused thoughtfully.

"But, anyway, my freshman year in college, a bunch of guys from my dorm were going out and asked me to go along. We went out to a pizza place downtown. We were goofing around at one of the pool tables having beers and this girl came over. She knew one of the guys, so he asked her to play. She ended up next to me and we played eight ball until our order was ready. When we went back to our booth she came along and I ended up stuck in the middle of the bench with her next to me. Everyone was talking and drinking and I guess I had a couple too many beers. I thought she was kind of pretty and since I was feeling no pain from the beers, when she asked me if I wanted to go for a walk, I said yes and we left. But, you know, if she hadn't asked me, I never would have had the guts to suggest it myself." A big sigh from him interrupted his story.

"We ended up at her apartment and she came on to me, kissing me and she took my shirt off. I felt like an idiot, not knowing what to do, you know?" He glanced at me, looking for some awareness from me of how he'd felt.

"I didn't know whether or where I should touch her. When she pulled me into her bedroom I was freaking out inside. We ended up on the bed and made out some more and then she took everything off but her underwear, so by then I'd gotten sort of hard. She took off her panties and I stripped off my shorts and got on top of her but I couldn't get it in. I couldn't find her vagina." His silence weighed heavily. "And my dick went limp."

He paused and sighed. He'd been looking at his knees the whole time, as he rushed through his story. He exhaled slowly, obviously dreading finishing his story. Then he sighed again with a shake of his head and continued.

"I tried kissing her some more, but I was so nervous I was sweating. I guess it's no surprise that nothing happened. Anyway, I rolled off and sat on the edge of the bed. She was nice about it and asked if I was okay, but I was too embarrassed to talk about it. I kind of blew her off, I guess. I threw my clothes on, said 'Sorry, and left." His voice trailed off and it was obvious that the memory was still painful, even after so much time.

"I'd see her every once in awhile after that, but I'd cross the street or go a different direction. I felt totally humiliated."

"I'm so sorry, that must have been really tough for you," I commiserated.

"Yeah, it was. Then the second time with another girl the same thing happened, only this time my dick kept getting soft and I fumbled around for so long she got frustrated, I guess, and said 'Never mind, let's just forget it'."

I didn't say anything in response, simply nodding my understanding.

"So ever since then, I've been afraid to even try. It feels like it's never going to work, but it works okay when I'm by myself, so I know there isn't anything wrong with me physically. It has to be in my head."

James' voice sounded a deep desperation and I felt a genuine compassion for him. I have heard variations of this theme many times. On the good side, I'd had a number of successes in working with clients to overcome it.

I reached out toward James but simply placed my hand on the sofa, not wanting to cause him more anxiety. "I know how hard it is to talk about this kind of thing, let alone to open up to someone you don't know.

That takes some courage and shows that you're ready to work on this and it's great that you're here James, to do that. There really is hope. There really is a light at the end of that tunnel."

Pulling my hand back and straightening a bit I asked, "So, do you know anything about this surrogate partner process?"

James shook his head, "No, not much really. Just the little bit that Dr. Johnston told me."

I settled in a little more comfortably into my sofa and inclined myself toward him just a bit, "Then let me tell you a little about the surrogate therapy model, with the understanding that this model is structured to suit you, who you are and what you're comfortable with in any given moment. We move at your pace. Although there is a model, it can go out the window any session, if the usual next step isn't working for us." When he nodded his understanding I went on.

"It's up to you to let me know if we're going to fast, or too slow or whether you're ready for the next thing. You are as much in control as I am and our key is to communicate with each other about what's going on with us, physically and emotionally. I need to hear how you're doing and I'll tell you how I'm doing as well. What we'll be doing is building a safe relationship for you to explore your sexuality."

"What do you mean by relationship?" James asked. "It's therapy, right?"

"Yes, it is therapy, but different from your relationship with your sex therapist. We'll be being physically *and* emotionally intimate with each other and between us, we'll try to model what a good relationship is. The boundary of our relationship is that it exists for two hours a week, or every other week, whatever our schedule is, and is not outside that time. It has a beginning, a middle and an end that will be determined by when you've met your goals."

At this point he appeared more interested than stressed, so I continued "Let me tell you about the model and we'll develop our relationship as we go along, if we decide to work together. The foundation of surrogate work is learning a way of touching our partner called sensate focus, or sensate caresses or self pleasuring touch. It involves paying such close attention to the sensations that you're experiencing, as the active partner who's touching the other, that you aren't thinking about anything else." James frowned a little, but nodded.

"You're not thinking about how your partner likes it, or if you're doing it right or how can you please her or what time it is, or your job or anything except the moment you're in, the feeling of her skin and finding ways to touch her that give *you* more sensation, more pleasure." I paused to let that sink in.

"It's a place to come back to when you lose awareness of your body, or you start worrying about your penis, or thinking too far ahead. The point is to just be in the moment with the sensations you're receiving. It's a training in being in your own body, and focusing on the sensations that are going on, so that your body can do what's natural, when it's pleasured."

James nodded again, although I knew he wouldn't be getting it yet.

I continued. "We work from the outside in, one at a time, one active partner and one passive partner doing hands and arms first. Then in another session we move on to faces, which often feels more vulnerable. When you feel comfortable with that, we then move on to explore feet and legs, or if it seems you're really doing well and I feel you're grounded in your own body, your own sensations, then we might get our clothes off. This happens over several sessions and each time we meet we'll decide together if we're ready to move on."

James looked a little concerned at this point. "How many sessions usually does it take before someone is done?" This is a question that always gets asked and for which there's no real answer, at least for me. It takes as long as each individual needs.

It's interesting to me. I doubt that most people ever ask their regular therapist that question, but when it comes to sexuality, one of the most important elements of their life, they expect a time limit. I felt my usual inner sigh, but since I knew that he didn't understand, I gave him the reply that I usually give: "There isn't any set time frame and a lot of it depends on how motivated you are, doing your homework and being willing to communicate. There's no quick fix. If there was, and I knew it, I'd be a rich woman."

Encouraged by his tight smile, I continued, "Anyway, after we get our clothes off," his involuntary flinch led me on to say, "and I do have a trick for that to make it easier, we'll do some mirror work. Each of us takes a turn looking at ourselves in the mirror and talking about how we feel about our body. This gets a lot of the discomfort about being naked with each other, out of the way, fast. Also, since I'll let you know how I feel about my hips or some scar, I don't have to wonder if you're secretly looking at them and maybe trying to avoid them, because you have the same feelings I do about them. It makes us more comfortable with each other naked, more quickly. From that point on, we do more sensate caresses on the back of the body, the front of the body, using exercises to teach you about the female anatomy, finding out what you like, what I like, on into all the things that will give you skills as a lover, and confidence."

I took a breath and waited a moment for all that to sink in. James looked as though he was giving it deep consideration.

I began again. "All that said, if what's on the schedule on any day isn't working for us, it's out and we'll do something else. So how does that all sound, so far?

Any questions for me at this point? I'm free to disclose a bit of information about myself and my own life, so you can ask me anything you want to and if I'm uncomfortable with it, I'll say so, okay?"

James frowned and thought about it for a minute and said "Well, I guess I do have a couple of questions." He looked around for a moment and then looked at me and said, "Would intercourse be an actual part of this? Because, I mean, I've had so much trouble with that."

"Well, let me say this; that there is no contract, no guarantee, of intercourse in this work. For a great many clients it might not be required, but my feeling is that everything that a person needs to make them a skilled and confident lover and partner should be covered. If that seems necessary, we'd talk about it at the time, and if we both agree, then we'd probably go there, but no intentions or commitments at this point. We'll have to see when we get to that point."

He took a breath and seemed relieved that although we would have the option, we weren't going to rush into anything.

"Okay, that sounds fair. It kind of takes the pressure off. The idea of doing it scares me, and not doing it scares me too. But I'm willing to wait and see. I guess the second thing I'd like to know is how long you've been doing this and what got you into it?"

CHAPTER 3
HOW I GOT INTO IT

People often ask me how I got into the work that I do and the reply that I give is usually a fairly general one, "Well, first of all, I've always been comfortable with my sexuality and when I moved to the Bay Area I was looking for a new direction for my life. At the beauty salon one day, I happened upon some articles about Surrogate Partner therapy in San Francisco magazine and thought "I bet I could do that.'" I did some investigating, found a training, received my certification and began my practice."

The real story has been constructed over many years of sexual exploration, four marriages (I began at sixteen) many lovers, some desperate one timers, full of yearning for love, and some profoundly intimate experiences, both sexual and deeply connected, to not only my partner, but myself as well.

Workshops helped me to explore both the spiritually powerful nature of sexuality and the playful, randy, even raunchy aspects. Spiritual teachers led me to the path of self-discovery, which would assist me in doing any deeply affecting personal work.

I'd been living in Los Angeles working in television as a unit manager for 11 years. I had a sweet little apartment in the Wilshire area, with tall French windows where my cats would sit, looking out on the city streets. My sons were no longer at home and I was living completely alone for the first time in my life except for the weekends, which were taken up in moments of sweet, hot passion with two different lovers.

LA was home to my spiritual community, my friends, family, my work- everything, it seemed was there.

As part of my spiritual quest, I had come up to do a day of LSD journey work with a shaman in the East Bay of the Bay area and was so impressed with the process that I found myself saying "If I lived here I could do this work more often."

Suddenly, in the way the Universe sometimes works, two weeks later I had a job offer from a station in San Francisco and a sublet apartment in the city, none of which I myself had sought out. All the events said go and all of a sudden I didn't want to. Everything I knew and loved was in Los Angeles.

The thought of leaving broke my heart but it seemed to me that if I didn't go, I would be resisting the flow of my life and a new opportunity. I've always believed that when these synchronicities occur, one should go for it. So in my forties, I gave up my darling little apartment with the French windows and the hot sweet memories of passion and love and drove, sobbing and snuffling to San Francisco, leaving behind my two lovers, my family and all my friends. I had never felt so alone and it was devastating.

I began working immediately in my new job only to discover that I hated not only the company I had come to work for, but also the job itself. I was bored with it all. After a few months, I managed to move from my sublet in the city to Mill Valley so at least my surroundings, among the redwoods and greenery, were beautiful.

It was during this time that I saw the articles in the magazine about a female and a male sexual surrogate partner and had an "ah-hah, I could do that!" realization. In that moment I remembered one balmy Southern California evening, lying in a cabin bed on a boat with a sometime lover, (one of those somewhat accomplished men who get that way by sleeping with a lot of women), basking in the afterglow, talking and touching.

He said something that filled my mind now. "You know, just laying with you feels like a healing." It was something I had felt, but had no words for. I began then to have a glimmer of my gift, but had no awareness at the time of how I might offer it to others, other than in my personal intimate relationships.

I know now that I am a sexual healer, one who uses the transformative power of sexual energy and a caring heart to heal. I know now also, that this journey was to heal myself as well, to bring myself to a place of self-acceptance, self-love and self-appreciation.

Reading the articles in the magazine I was intrigued, and had an epiphany as to how I could change my life. I made note of the information and the next day began making calls to see how one goes about learning to be a surrogate. A call to The Institute for the Study of Human Sexuality got me the number for IPSA, the International Professional Surrogates Association.

I called the organization for information about classes, filled out the extensive application and mailed it in. It was an anxious wait but my acceptance came in a few weeks. I then had to wait until enough people for a class formed (which took awhile given that not too many look to do this work), but finally headed for Los Angeles for my two-week training, both excited and filled with trepidation.

"What if I can't do this after all? And even more than that, what will I be expected to do and with whom?" my little conservative side mumbled.

I was glad that I was able to stay with my friend Rae at her home in Los Angeles as I had anticipated some intense work packed into twelve days and knew that I would need some fun and a perspective on myself as only a good friend can offer. I had really missed her since my move, so it would be good to have the time to catch up and her home held lots of memories of fabulous parties and dream workshops we'd done together. The night of my arrival we sat up talking about everyone we knew, where they were and what they were doing, our laughter and ease with each other relaxing some of my nervousness.

The next morning I drove to the meeting place. Vena greeted me at the door with welcoming smile set in a face I knew I would come to love. I recognized her voice from my conversations with the Association. She was in her mid thirties, small and pretty in a very natural way, with a light brown, soft bob. Not a Playboy bunny, but a lovely personable woman, a regular person, like me, doing this work. I was aware that she would be one of my trainers and I wondered that since she looked so young how long could she possibly have been practicing?

She ushered me in to a room that was comfortable enough, though with no particular style of décor.

There was an easel set up to one side against a wall, and there were a few other people sitting on the sofa and in chairs around the area.

Vena introduced me to the others: first came Alex, a tall, slender fellow with curly, sandy hair who seemed foreign, a slight accent giving him away. Then came VJ, Vena's sister, also a trainer, a little darker hair, attractive, but like most of us, no centerfold, with the same friendly smile as her sister. Lastly, a guy named Terry. He was short, slender, dark haired, with a generally disheveled look, clad in a pair of worn Levis and a wrinkled t-shirt.

Everyone made small talk, telling one another why we were there while we waited for the other attendees and the other trainer to arrive. Alex said he had chosen to attend the training in the hopes of becoming a surrogate and Terry admitted that he was there simply to learn some skills and gain some confidence in himself and his abilities as a lover.

A knock on the door gave entrance to a very pretty, red haired young woman who introduced herself as Hannah. She seemed easy and confident in her body and was dressed in a bohemian fashion that screamed sexuality workshops. I had a moment of dread and wondered if I was too old to be starting this, but let that thought go as quickly as I could. My instincts told me that I had something to offer and I hoped that I would find a vehicle for that here.

The other participant Lori, a slender, attractive woman in her 40's, with straight brown hair and warm eyes, arrived shortly after Hannah and was followed closely by the other trainer Larry.

Oh, Larry! It was instant lust and longing on my part. Tall, with black hair and exotic features, sweetly curved full lips and a deliciously relaxed, sensual way about him: Obviously, a bit of a bad boy, a sweet bad boy. My downfall every time, at the time!

His olive skin looked as though it would feel like silk. All my sensors were on high volume the moment I looked at him and I wanted to rub up against him. And more! Lots more!

My attraction for him was to become one of my areas of personal work during the training. Boundaries! I felt an intense attraction for him, but the integrity of the work demanded that I set it aside.

He did say at one time during the training, when we worked an exercise together, "Oh, another time, another place." I understood exactly what he meant and we both laughed.

I was pleased and pleasantly surprised at how normal the trainers were. They were also all practicing surrogates themselves. Vena was married with a daughter, and VJ and Larry were single. I felt very welcomed by all of them. They were very professional, but open and warm. Vena in particular seemed to be a giant heart, combined with a delightful sense of humor and a fine mind and I felt a strong rapport with her.

I knew that all the psychological and transpersonal work I had done up to this point, along with my love of exploration would hold me in good stead in the training.

We were to work with the same person all through the training. We were evenly paired in male/female couples, as if our partners were clients, while we learned to follow the surrogate therapy model. I was paired with Terry, a nice enough, rather meek but amenable guy, and absolutely not anyone I would have been interested in out in the world.

He may have felt the same way about me, as well, but by the time we said good-bye, we had been through a relationship together and had achieved a sense of closeness. That's something that happens most of the time in surrogate therapy and it comes out of the relationship I establish with my client and transcends any immediate physical or emotional attraction.

I felt sexy and knowledgeable during the training, even though the work was exhausting at times and challenging. Long hours everyday were divided between lectures of a psychological nature, physiology and sexual functioning and practicing exercises in sensate focus, which I've described previously. It felt so natural to me that I felt as though I'd been training for this all my life with every lover. As we proceeded, we dealt with issues of body image, how to work with the physical and emotional aspects of sexual dysfunction, exercises to establish trust, various sexual techniques and enhancement. Who knew that eating cucumbers could cause body fluids to taste sweet! We shared feelings, kept notes and were sent home to journal our thoughts each day. We learned how to deal with difficult issues with a client by dealing with issues that arose with our partner.

We all watched Hannah and her partner struggle together, recognizing that she was bringing her own neediness into her work with him. The result being that she blamed him for being uncaring and not attending to her feelings. The trainers worked with the two of them but it was clear that she couldn't hear what the rest of us could see. Her own baggage, the issues she needed to work on, was exaggerated by the closeness and intimacy of the work. Because she hadn't done her own healing in those areas, she projected onto her partner making him, in her mind, the uncaring bad guy. He felt alternately perplexed, sad and angry and we all felt sorry for both of them. The tension made us all uncomfortable, but their ability to be vulnerable in the group gave all of us a chance to have a good look at ourselves.

I kept checking myself throughout the training. Could I maintain my own emotional health and not project my needs onto my clients? It's a critical part of the emotional maturity required to do this work. I felt comfortable with that idea and for the most part, in my practice, it's been true.

I was presented in my own training relationship with a problem that required some caring honesty. One of the most uncomfortable problems to address with any client is the issue of hygiene and I had to deal with that very thing with my partner. Terry was scruffy and unkempt. His clothes were not always clean and while his body wasn't terribly offensive, when he tossed his underwear on the floor, brown marks in them shocked and disgusted me.

After a counseling session with the trainers, it became clear that I needed to talk to him about it. All of a sudden he felt like a complete and total stranger and not someone that I'd been sharing intimate time with for the last week, but now that we were entering the more erotic part of our training, it became a necessity to speak to him about it.

After receiving some support from my trainers, I finally had a talk with him. He came to our next session unshaven and it gave me the opportunity to tell him how important cleanliness was to me. I said I would really appreciate his shaving and pointed out that I always took care to come to sessions with him clean and fresh and in clean clothes as well. I told him that it would mean a lot to me if he would take a little more care as we're working together.

He took it quite well, saying that he actually didn't shower very often and just grabbed whatever clothes were handy. He seemed a little embarrassed, but assured me that he would shower and change underwear every day from then on. After that it became much easier for me to be close to him.

I don't remember if kissing was part of the training as well, but also don't recall if we went there. I do however, remember being concerned with his oral hygiene. On the other hand, I've often charged into the uncomfortable, so we may have, but I can say that it definitely wasn't memorable.

In the two weeks of training we covered each step of the surrogate therapy model, from the sensate focus, non-demand touching, to discovering our erogenous zones. We learned what our sexual and sensual likes and dislikes were, how to work with different sexual dysfunctions, both male and female, the importance of communicating feeling with honesty and connecting and creating and modeling healthy relationship.

I came to a place of real appreciation for my "client" partner, for his willingness to step up and do the work with me. After all, he had only had sex in "massage parlors" or nude encounter groups and had never been involved in any deeply caring, loving relationships. He was an emotional and relational innocent and needed guidance from the ground up and I was pleased that I was able to provide some of this for him.

One of my personal challenges in the training was the journaling requirement. We had been instructed to journal about our experience every night. Our journals were read and commented upon every day by the trainers and we were expected to write down all our feelings regarding ourselves, and our "client." Talk about feeling vulnerable! That also meant my writing about my feelings for sexy Larry in a forum that he would read. All the trainers took it in stride, including him (I'm sure it must have happened before).

I also had the opportunity to talk about my crush on him in person as well and by the end of the training I had managed to lose the longing for him and still keep those yummy, wanton feelings. The lust was good and understandable, given my taste in luscious bad boys, but the longing hadn't been reasonable, as I didn't really know him.

I came to understand that an old childhood pattern of needing to be seen, loved and cherished by a man (my father had been away a lot) had been activated and my ability to talk about it and discuss it in that safe setting became a tremendous opportunity to separate the attraction from the longing. It was the beginning of a healing for me as it also helped me to see that particular issue as having been a motivator for me in previous attractions.

By the time I had been there a few days, I knew that I was up to the challenge inherent in surrogate work. I also was profoundly grateful for all the hard personal work I had done and for all the loving relationships I had had, as well as all the ones that ended in misery. They had all been my teachers.

I had the opportunity to witness the other trainees working in their "relationships" and saw that we all had our moments of difficulty. For me, it was a validation of all the past personal work I had done that I graduated from the training with an unqualified pass to establish an internship with a client, a therapist and a mentor, receive certification and go on to begin my practice. Sometimes surrogate trainees are referred for more of their own therapy or to do some more training before they are actually certified. Some, unfortunately, might not make it at all.

On reaching the end of the training, Terry and I had developed a relative fondness for each other, born it felt, out of the discomfort of our honesty and vulnerability. We had finally developed a relationship and one that I hoped would be a model for him in the future. We agreed to be in contact at some point post-graduation, after a period of separation, just to see how the other was doing, but actually were in contact only once. It was enough.

I returned home and was able to find a therapist willing to supervise my first case, a young man in his twenties from Australia, here for a couple of months, a virgin, who, in a kissing session, said to me, "I've never kissed an elderly person before." Actually, though a good deal older than him, I certainly wasn't elderly and he'd never kissed anyone before.

It was a difficult and challenging case, involving arousal difficulties and the time that he had with me before resuming his travels was much too short to address all the emotional and psychological issues surrounding his problem. We had made a lot of progress, but when he returned the book on male sexuality that I had given him to keep, because he was afraid someone might see it in his van, it was definitely a comment on his psychological state surrounding sexuality.

All in all however, I felt we had done a lot of good work together, and had discovered avenues of arousal for him. It was a good, if incomplete, start.

I came into this work with an ability to be physically intimate, to be skin to skin in an open hearted, accepting way, but being vulnerable has been and is an on going lesson and work in progress.

Communication, letting my partner see me at my most human, nervous myself, concerned about my body, a person with feelings, not just a therapist, allows them to be vulnerable as well.

Modeling a good relationship is as important as any of the physical work that I do with a client. Each person that I work with is a relationship, and knowing and accepting that it has that beginning, middle, and end makes us more present in the moment. We know the parameters, the boundaries and within those boundaries is hopefully, ultimately a sense of ease. It takes awhile to get to that place of ease, however.

The person sitting opposite me on the couch in the first session is generally nervous, anxious and often hardly breathing so we start there, with breath. Deep relaxing breaths into the belly and when he or she is more comfortable, we begin to talk. I'm finding out about him or her, taking a history, what brought them here, what their goals are. However the problem is expressing, physically, emotionally or socially, the result is generally an inability to begin, or sustain a loving, sexual relationship and this is what I most care about.

I believe that all humans want connection, and relationship is the most essential part of what it is to be human, and not entering into relationship should be able to come from choice, not from a feeling of inability, or paralyzing fear.

If I can help someone find ways to deal with their physical problem, allay their fears, give them skills and some confidence, and show them the rewards of a loving sexual relationship, their life can be dramatically changed.

I see the results of our work, not just in my living room, or the bedroom but, in a client's social interactions in the world. A person's hidden, secret feelings about their sexuality bleed out into their life in ways that one wouldn't ordinarily think of; "better not talk to that woman I like or she might expect me to get things going with her and I don't know how or, it won't work." Or "I'm not a real man," or "It's too hard to have friends. They might wonder why I don't date and how would I explain it?" or "No sense keeping my house clean, no one will ever see it." There could be a general sense of unworthi-ness.

On the other hand the client may be very success-ful in their work, because that's all they ever do. I have had some clients that were adept socially, but never cul-tivated any close personal relationships, skimming the surface, never staying too long with any one person, never sharing anything personal for fear of exposure.

Some clients have had decent sexual relationships in the past but, for one of many possible reasons, be-gin to have problems getting or maintaining erections, ejaculating too quickly or not at all.

Occasionally, one comes that has been married for many years and finds themselves divorced and com-pletely unsure of how to go about meeting partners, dating and initiating intimate relationships.

For all of these people, I become their partner in discovery, their coach, their confidante, their truth teller, their lover, and yes, their friend. It's a relation-ship that exists within the confines of our 2 hours to-gether each or every other week. To this extent, I feel that the words surrogate partner are a misnomer, for during the time that we are together in our work, we are real partners, doing our best to model a good relationship, with support, honesty and caring. We're just not out in the world together, and as I have said, we know that our relationship will end when our work is finished.

This is what James and I will attempt to build together and our journey is just beginning.

CHAPTER 4

JAMES-FIRST SESSION CONTINUED

After I gave James, my usual answer about my comfort with sexuality, my move to the Bay Area and my discovery of surrogate therapy, his next question was "Have you had, I mean, can you tell me what you think your success rate is?"

This question is often asked and although I understand it, I can't accurately answer it because there isn't any way to rate it. I've had some clients begin relationships while in therapy (which I encourage, so that we can address problems that arise), others have finished therapy and gone on to establish them, some have left just feeling better about themselves and more able to function socially. Most learn to work with or control their problems, and a few don't quite achieve their goals

Sometimes even though a particular goal has been accomplished, the client will find that other, new goals arise, with more discoveries to be made. Most clients tell me that what they get out of the work is a hundred times more than they ever thought or expected.

I explained all this to James and added that his inexperience was my favorite problem to work with. Although there are always underlying issues with which we'd need to deal, there are also usually wonderful surprises for both of us.

He smiled, nodded. "Well, that's good to hear, I guess."

"So, do you have any more questions for me?"

He looked thoughtful for a moment, then said, "I don't think so. Not right now, anyway. I'll probably have more later."

"Well, we'll find out a lot about each other as we go along, if we decide to work together and if anything comes up we'll deal with it as it arises. And speaking of that, how are you feeling about that idea? Do you feel comfortable enough to work with me? I am a good deal older than you, which might matter to some people, so I need to know if you have any problem with that?"

James shook his head and said "No, it's not a problem for me and yes, I do feel comfortable with you."
He paused and went on. "How about you, are you comfortable with me?"

I felt a sense of relief because the age issue is sometimes a touchy one. If a client stays, it usually ends up
not mattering. I've had clients who expressed concern
in the beginning and by the middle of the process, began to see me only as their "fire woman," their sexual
healer and teacher.

"Yes, I am, James and I think I can help you," I
smiled. "Well good, it seems as if we've decided, so we
can go into our second hour and begin the first of the
exercises, okay?" I was feeling confident and ready to
get started.

I rose to my feet. "Would you mind helping me
move the coffee table?"

James nodded "Sure, no problem." He got up as
well, and we moved the table across the living room
so that we could unfold the rectangular pale green futon that I keep against a wall. I always work my first
few sessions in the living room, before going up to the
guest room. It's more comfortable for me, until we get
to know each other and also most of my clients seem
to appreciate not being overwhelmed by the idea of
the looming bed. It's definitely less threatening in the
living room until we get past the first awkwardness of
therapy.

My living room is warm and welcoming with it's rich, burgundy area rug and buttery walls and once I pull the burgundy drapes to the garden it becomes an intimate space. It's quite comfortable on the futon on the floor, with pillows as props. For me it's a sacred space, made by our intention to create intimacy and privacy.

James wore a short sleeve shirt, allowing me access to his bare arms, so I invited him to remove his watch and gestured that he should take a seat in the middle of the futon.

I am always the active partner first. This serves primarily as a teaching experience for the client, so that he will have an understanding of the process and also so that he will have some awareness of how his partner might feel when he is doing the caressing.

"Why don't you lie back on the pillows and make yourself comfortable," I encouraged.

He tried, given his anxiety of the moment, and nervously plumped the mint and forest green pillows, rearranging them, moving them around, moving them again, trying his head on one and moving it and trying his head on another and finally coming to a tentative stop with his fingers tightly interlaced on his chest. His jaw was clenched and I could see a tiny muscle twitch. His anxiety was also betrayed by the tension in his body and his short and shallow, breathing.

I sat down on the futon next to him, but facing him. "Take a deep breath James," I reminded him gently.

While all clients are nervous, some are more so than others. Some are able to take these first sessions in their stride but face their anxieties and resistances later when the issues that have brought them to therapy really begin to surface. James had so little experience that almost everything we would do together would be a jump into the unknown. This is my favorite kind of client and I understand that this is a sacred trust, a potentially life changing process for this man lying rigidly on my futon. Hopefully, together, we'd create a space for his healing….and some fun and pleasure along with it.

"Why don't you close your eyes now James and try to relax a bit. I'm just going to take you through some breathing exercises right now."

He obediently closed his eyes and burrowed a little deeper into the futon, placing his arms at his sides.

"Okay, so take some good deep breaths James and see if you can breathe into your belly. Imagine the breath moving past the lungs and into the abdomen, so that *it* rises and falls instead of the chest."

I watched his belly expand with his breath. "Good, James, that's it," I encouraged. I watched him for several minutes until I could see his jaw relaxing slightly and some tension drifting away.

Speaking quietly I said, "Now James, let go of thinking about breathing and just let your breath move
deeply, but naturally. I'm going to take you through a
meditation for relaxation and awareness of sensation."

I paused a moment and then began, speaking softly. "Imagine that your breath is moving through your
body all the way down to your feet. It fills your toes
and moves through the bones and tissue and they become soft and heavy. See if you can feel that heaviness,
the feet sinking into the futon, the ankle bones turning liquid and dripping into the fabric beneath them."
I gave him a few moments and then moved his focus
into his calves and around his knees and up his thighs.

I continued this way, all the way up his body, guiding him into relaxation, but also into a general awareness of any sensation that his body could experience
without any movement, like temperature differences
or feelings of heaviness or lightness. At the conclusion, his body looked softly relaxed and his breaths
were easy. I then began to take him through a short
sensate meditation.

"Alright James, I want you now to let yourself remain relaxed, while you focus on some different sensations. I'd like you to see if you can feel the weight
of your shirt or pants on your body. Maybe you can
feel your shirt move with your breath, or maybe you
can feel the weight of your belt." I gave him time to

explore whatever awareness he had of those general sensations.

"When you're ready, feel free to move one hand on the futon, just noticing what sensations you experience."

He rubbed his hand slowly. "See if you can feel a temperature difference between where your hand was and another place, or if you also touch your shirt after the futon, the difference in the sensation of the textures." He gathered the corner of his shirt and rubbed it between his thumb and forefinger and then rubbed his fingertips on the futon.

"Just notice any sensations for yourself. You can tell me later. Now, focus on inside of your mouth. Feel where your tongue is resting. Does your mouth feel warm or does it change as you breathe. Is there a taste in your mouth that you can sense? Running your tongue over the back of your teeth, can you feel the tiny spaces in between?" I could tell from his cheeks that he was exploring the inner realms of his mouth.

"Now, bring your attention to your nose. As you breathe, notice the temperature difference between the in breath and the out breath. What can you smell? The ambient smell of the room or maybe perfume or maybe yourself, your clothes. Just focusing on what smells are present." There was just the slightest hint of a movement of his brows that told me he was concentrating.

"Leaving your nose now, focus your attention on what you're hearing. What different sounds are you aware of? Can you hear your own breathing? Or, my breathing? Imagine your ears like a cat, turning your ears this way and that, to pick up the smallest sound, even those far away." James smiled, a bare quirk of the corner of his mouth. I stayed quiet again, letting him enjoy the exploration of his ears.

"Now let's move up to your eyes. Keeping them closed, just notice the awareness of light and dark, or of any changing colors or patterns. What are the insides of your eyelids like? You can place your hand over one eye to notice the contrast, if you like." He brought his hand up to cup his right eye and I could see his left eye moving back and forth beneath the lid. "When you're done with that, just relax again and see if you can experience what's going on in your whole body, sounds, smells, temperature, any sensation."

His hand returned to its place on the futon and he sighed a long sigh…a good sign.

"These sensations are being experienced by our body all the time James, but when we're in our head or not present in our body, we're not aware of them, that's all. So, you can open your eyes when you're ready and tell me how you're feeling." I waited silently and after a minute or so, he opened his eyes and turned his head to look at me, his brown eyes calm and dreamy.

"That was nice. I feel heavy, but really good."

"And how was the experience of sensation for you?"

"Well, it's interesting to think that I don't feel stuff most of the time. I'm just not aware of it, I guess. It seems like I don't pay much attention to my body, unless it hurts for some reason. But, it was all very relaxing and easy. I liked it."

"Good. You seemed very relaxed. That's a great beginning to our next exercise.

Are you ready?" He nodded, swallowing slightly. "I'm going to touch your hand then." I reached over and put my hand on his. The back of his hand was dry and cool, but the palm, where my fingertips were curling into it, was damp with instantaneous nerves.

"I'm ready to begin James, does this feel alright, my hand on yours?" I was in charge, but conscious of the fact that he probably hadn't been touched much in his life, other than handshakes and certainly not intimately.

When he nodded, I described the way I would touch him, told him that I would be paying close attention to what his skin felt like: the texture, the temperature, the differences from one place to another. I would be a body explorer of his hand and arm, searching for interesting things, as though he were a landscape I had never been to and wanted to know. I would find ways to enjoy myself, to play, to take pleasure in this landscape and if my mind should wander, to come back to it. His only task was to relax into it as best he could and to take deep, calming breaths if he felt anxious.

I knew that all of this was a foreign language to him, but when I was finished, he would definitely have a better sense of what I was talking about. I closed my eyes, took a moment to drop into being present, bringing my focus, with my breath, into the moment at hand and began to run one hand slowly up his arm. It usually takes a few minutes of attention, to reach the point where I am no longer an observer of the sensations I'm having, but am immersed in them, fully sensual. I use my hand, the inside of my own arm against theirs and occasionally, if I sense they are relaxed enough, my cheek.

At the start of my work with a new client, I do not enter as fully into the experience as I might at another time. As their guide I need to be aware of how the client is doing, as well as demonstrating the possibilities of sensate touch.

I lifted James' hand and felt his arm tense reflexively, holding it up. I interrupted my excursion to ask him to relax his arm. He tried, but when I dropped his hand suddenly, it remained for a moment in the air before he let it down. This is pretty normal; an often unconscious instinct to control their body or do something "helpful", and usually becomes easier as a client learns to trust, let go and receive sensual touch.

"Don't worry, you'll get the hang of it," I assured him. I picked his hand and arm up again and held them up. "I'd like you to imagine that your arm is a dishrag, heavy and full with water, so that when I let go it'll just flop. You don't have to help me or do anything at all, but see if you can just let it go. Okay?" I picked his hand up again and he was trying, but it took us several tries to get any flop at all.

"You'll get there James. We'll work on it," I reassured him. Then I refocused and began again.

I spent a few minutes becoming acquainted with his arm, discovering the softness of the skin along the inner side and the coarser covering of skin and hair on the outer. I glided my finger into the curve of his elbow down the soft veins to his wrist bone and slowly, I began to feel the deep connection with sensation that happens with this process. This is when the exercise becomes a caring but sensual dance for me of hands, arms and heart.

Because James had probably been touch deprived, it took awhile for him to relax and enjoy it, but I noticed that his breathing became more natural at some point and there may have even been a small sound of appreciation from him. After spending 15 or twenty minutes experiencing both arms, I sat quietly, waiting for him to come up for air, giving him time to assimilate everything he'd felt, and to get himself together.

When I saw his brown eyes open and look sideways at me I asked "So how was that for you?"

"Relaxing," he replied. A standard answer, because at this point he probably didn't have any words at hand to describe what he felt.

"Can you tell me how the touch felt to you and can you use descriptive words, like soft or hard?"

"Well," he looked thoughtfully at me, "it was soft and sometimes it tickled a little, like on the inside of my arm. Did you rub my arm on your cheek?" I nodded.

"I liked that. It felt kind of weird, but I liked it."

"Anything else?" I asked.

"Yeah, I felt your hair brush my arm and I liked that too."

"Could you tell what I was doing, other than that?"

"No, not really. I think I sort of drifted in and out some, but it felt really nice. I've never felt anything like that."

"Well, It's a different way of being touched and even people that are used to touching, haven't usually experienced it this way. Ordinarily, when someone spends time touching someone else, it's for the one *being* touched, either to make them feel good or to excite them or something else along those lines. And that's okay. There are times when that's appropriate, but I can tell you from experience that when you're really enjoying someone's body, they enjoy it too. I think it's a gift, to let someone know this way how much you love their body, that you get pleasure touching them. I know it makes me feel beautiful and sexy. And my body and my being respond that way."

I gave him a moment to digest this idea. "How about your feelings, the emotional ones, I mean. Were you aware of any of those types of feelings?"

"Well, I felt comfortable and the way you touched me felt like, I don't know, maybe caring? It felt like you cared about me and maybe that you liked it, too?"

"Exactly," I answered, I enjoyed it too. I felt a connection to you, so I'm glad you felt that." We exchanged smiles. "So, ready to take your turn with me?" I asked.

"Yeah, I guess so, but I don't really know what I'm doing. I guess I'm a little nervous, my hands feel sticky."

"No problem" I said, getting up. "I'll get some powder. That'll help a lot."

When I returned from the bathroom with the powder, James was sitting on the edge of the futon, looking very uneasy, so I plopped down in the middle casually and handed him the powder. "Powder feels nice anyway. It's smooth and smells good. It'll let you enjoy the experience a little more."

I made myself comfortable in the center and James shook some powder into his hand and rubbed his hands together, while I took a deep breath of the soft familiar scent and relaxed. "Ready?" he asked.

"Um hmm, ready," I replied and he took my hand tentatively, and cruised his other hand up and down my forearm. I stopped him, saying gently, "James, wait a minute. Before you begin, I want you to take a couple of deep breaths into your belly and try to relax. Just focus on what your hand is telling you. You don't have to use just your fingers. It's okay to use other parts of your hand, like your palm. You can also use the back of your hand as well, or the inside of your forearm, anyway that you can think of to get more and different sensations. If you find your mind wandering, come back to your breath; breathe into your belly and focus on your hand and my arm." James nodded and took another deep breath.

"Try to stay away from wondering if you're doing it right. There isn't any right way, just the ways that are enjoyable for you. If I'm uncomfortable, I'll say so, otherwise, have a good time. I'm pretty good at knowing when someone has gone into their head or is wandering away in their thoughts, so if I feel that, I'll call you back, okay?"

He took a deep inhalation. "Mmh, okay," he sighed. I closed my eyes as he began to run his hand up my arm.

He didn't do too badly, considering that this was a brand new experience. Once or twice I caught his mind wandering and reminded him to breathe and come back to sensations. Repetitive stroking in the same spot is a dead giveaway that a client has gone someplace else or is thinking too much. He explored a little with using his forearm and once, even stroked my arm with his cheek. Brave on his part, as a beginner. He stopped a couple of times to add powder, when his hands began stopping and starting on my arm like a beginner trying to drive a car with a clutch, but all in all a good beginning.

When he was finished, I asked him how it had felt for him.

I was nervous," he admitted, "But it did feel good to know that I could touch someone. You know, and enjoy it."

"That's really good. And can you tell me about any thing you noticed? Any specific things your hand or arm felt? You know, any tactile sensations you were particularly aware of?"

"Well, your skin felt soft and warm. I did notice that it's smoother and warmer on the inside of your arm and especially your elbow, than the outside of your arm: Maybe because of the little hairs on the outside? I really felt those with my face, but they were pretty soft. I don't know… I feel like I wasn't always totally there, but I tried to keep paying attention."

"Great, it's a terrific start, don't you think? For someone who hasn't really touched anyone?"

"Yeah, I guess so." He gave a small shrug, looking tentatively pleased.

"So how did it feel to you? Was it okay?" His question was hopeful.

"I enjoyed it a lot, even though I could feel you disappearing once in awhile. But you always came right back when I asked you to breathe. Overall, I felt like you were pretty much present in the experience most of the time. It's a good beginning and I promise it'll get better. Every time we practice sensate touch it will be easier and more enjoyable for you."

"Great, I hope so. It just all feels so new, you know?"

"Yes, I know, but trust me, time and practice make it more natural."

"I know, but....I'm trying to believe that." He lay down on his side facing me, his hand supporting his head. He looked down pensively and fingered the edge of a pillow. "Could I ask you something personal?"

I nodded. "Sure, of course. I'll answer it if I can. I can tell you as much as I'm comfortable with at this point. What is it?"

"Well, from your ring, it looks like you're married?"

I nodded again, "Yes, you're right, I am."

Looking a little concerned, he asked "Well, how does your husband feel about you doing this? Is this okay with him?" His look said he didn't understand how it could be so.

"Yeah! He is absolutely okay with it. I know most men would probably have difficulty with this work, but it might interest you to know though, there are other married surrogate partners. It's not unique."

"Really." James nodded and his eyebrows went up as he absorbed the information.

"He and I speak only generally about my work, but he definitely knows what it's all about and he supports me completely. So, does that feel okay with you? Or does it cause you a lot of concern?"

James shrugged, "No I guess not. As long as he's really okay with my being here, I guess I'm okay with it, too."

"Good!" I smiled, "You'll have to trust me on that one, it really is okay. So, if we're clear on that, is there anything else?"

"No, that's it. I noticed your ring last time and I've been thinking about it, so I'm glad that I asked. I'm cool with it. It's fine." He sat up as if to punctuate his assertion.

Our time was winding down, but I gave James homework to do before our next meeting, the following week. I assigned him sensate touch on himself, on any parts that he could reach, including his genitals, if he wished, but not with masturbation in mind. The purpose was to simply explore his own body, to pay attention to sensation and pleasure as both the receiver and the explorer. Also, I asked him to practice on other things, stroking animals or objects or fabrics to develop an awareness of texture.

His other homework was to practice breathing, drawing air into his belly and noticing not only his breath, but the sensations it produced in his body. It's a great grounding and relaxing exercise to use, not only as we were using it, but in the world as well, when one is anxious or agitated. I asked him to spend a few minutes practicing that upon waking and before sleeping each day.

With that, I saw James to the door, seeing him off with a warm hug, which I requested, and sent him out into the world with, I hoped, a little new sense of wonder with himself.

CHAPTER 5
MY HUSBAND

When I tell people that I make my living as a surrogate partner, most of them usually glaze over, look confused and say "Really!" meaning either, "what's that?" or more often, "aren't you a little old to be having babies for people?" Then, because I know they don't know, I ask, "Do you know what surrogate partners do?" they reply with something like "I guess not," or "well I thought I did, but…"

So, I then give my usual clinical explanation; that I work with therapists and their clients that are sexually or emotionally dysfunctional. I explain that the therapist does the talk therapy and I serve as the partner, doing the intimate hands on therapy, which encompasses all aspects one would encounter in a relationship. Although some are uncomfortable with the topic, most are intrigued and ask a lot of questions.

When they notice the ring on my left hand, they often ask "and you're married?" with some disbelief. "How does your husband feel about it?"

My answer is that I am married to a wonderful man, who honors my gifts of service and the work that I do. Besides, I was doing this work when we met, so he knew what he would be getting into when he asked me out. He has never asked me to stop and has only supported and encouraged me. He is respectful of the work and understands the value of it.

I am privileged to be able to have both this meaningful work and a personal and private relationship with my husband that is meaningful as well. I am so grateful to have the love and stability of my marriage with someone of my own who supports me, who really sees me and cares for me as I am. He truly appreciates my gifts, and loves me because of them, not in spite of them.

I met my future husband in the foyer of my friend Irene's house where he was visiting her room-mate, his ex-girlfriend, at the end of their session of body painting, as I recall. Something that certainly made a statement to me about how open he was. It didn't hurt that I found him quite handsome, with his dark brown hair and warm eyes, and sexy, as I admired her artwork on his strong, well formed body. Our meeting was brief, but the spark, the chemistry was immediate and lasting, enough for me to ask questions about him to the ex-girlfriend, later.

Apparently he was doing the same because after that, every time I visited there, his ex-girlfriend happily became the messenger between us, providing information, to and from each of us. She told me more about him and answered my questions about what he did, what he was like, the things he enjoyed and telling me how pretty and sexy he thought I was. It all felt very teen-age like, but delightful, and a little embarrassing to realize that I had a schoolgirl crush at this stage in my life.

She was also doing the same for him; relaying to him what she knew about me, my profession, and my attraction to him, in response to his questions. She told me he found my career fascinating.

He and I saw each other a few times at parties, but he had a relationship at the time, so we didn't pursue our interest. A few months after that he began attending a class I taught about using movement for personal growth and creativity. The feelings were still there, but we danced around our attraction to each other. He was still in relationship and besides, because he was in my class, it didn't feel appropriate anyway. I was the teacher and he was the student.

He even brought his girlfriend to class once. But, because he was such a good dancer, it made me dream of having a relationship with a man I would be able to dance with. "How wonderful that would be," I thought.

I got to know him better over a year, as the students and I often had pizza after class, but it was after the class ended and the ending of his relationship, before we started dating. I had a tremendous amount of trepidation at first because he's a number of years younger than me and I had doubts about a relationship with such disparity in age.

"What am I getting myself into?" I worried. "What will people say?" I fretted.

Well, our friends said "Hooray!" and others simply got used to us. Now, we've been together eighteen years and married for ten, so it seems to be working and we are happy and productive together.

People who don't know us well, sometimes ask me or us, how he does it. How he can be okay with the fact that his wife engages sensually, or sexually with others. The answer is that he's comfortable with his own sexuality, and trusts our relationship enough to not be threatened by my work.

He's extraordinarily open-minded and he believes that emotional and physical relationships are powerful and important for every human being. His feeling is that if I can help heal social and psychic wounds in that area, then it's important that I do so. He is also aware that actual sexuality is only a small part of the work that I do.

As a scientist, his work every day demands that he be able to compartmentalize and in this situation, this ability works well for both of us. According to him, when he considers my work, it helps to be a scientist, a clinical person, rather than a romantic (although he certainly is that as well, sometimes).

He tells me that he trusts my boundaries; that I will adhere to the limits I have set regarding the separation between my relationship with him and our home, and that of the client and myself. He trusts that if I were to begin to have any difficulty with those guidelines, I'd say something.

If my boundaries were not clear in my work it would be a problem, for both of us. When I ask him about it, he says that because of the teaching, healing and clinical aspect of my work, he actually has less fear about my falling in love or leaving him for one of my clients, than if I were to meet someone outside of the work.

When people ask my husband why he copes with my job, his answer is straightforward and to the point: "This is who she is and if I asked her to stop, I'd be asking her to be less than herself," and that a big part of what he loves about me is my openness, my sense of freedom and my ability to heal others. He also tells them that he doesn't ask about my work, except whether or not a session went well. He appreciates that I don't tell him anything about my clients as he really doesn't want to know anyway.

I don't tell him about my clients or our sessions, as my work is confidential, like any therapist, but I do use him occasionally to get a man's viewpoint of a situation. His response, of course, comes from one who has little damage in the area of sexuality, but his comments and insights around male emotional issues are generally quite helpful.

I am blessed to have such a great life partner, and I am not alone in recognizing this. At a dinner meeting of therapists, surrogates and guests, a female therapist leaned over to my handsome husband and said "You must be an amazing man!" and I agree with her completely.

He's not the only extraordinary spouse, of course. As I told James, a number of female surrogates are married. We're pretty normal people, more open than many perhaps, but regular people with full lives outside of our work. Other than my practice, we're a pretty regular, active, loving couple.

To maintain and nurture our relationship, we participate in a couples support group. It provides a safe place for each couple to work through shared problems, and have those issues witnessed by supportive friends, while receiving as much feedback as we want. All of them know about my work and love and support, not only our relationship, but also each of us individually. My profession however, is generally not a topic of discussion in our work together as a couple. We have plenty of the same kind of other issues to work on that any couple in relationship would have.

My husband and I didn't arrive at our current state of understanding without mishaps. Mostly in the earlier stages of our relationship, I was a little careless occasionally and missed small things, like a condom wrapper on the floor or the Astroglide lubricant left out in my workroom. Naturally, those missteps were uncomfortable for both of us. When confronted with them, I could only apologize and listen to his expression of anger, his feelings that I was not protecting our relationship. As much as he respected my work, he did not want to feel as though I was flaunting it in his face.

As we would talk our way through it, I certainly became much more careful, keeping the supplies and things I use in my work separate from our personal lives.

This is one of our most critical boundaries, and it is important to him that it be honored, as it is to me as well, to keep my work very separate from our life together. We want to keep our home *our* home, a sacred space in its own right. I have my surrogate supplies in one location and we have our own personal supplies of intimate items in another and they never cross over. Aside from my work, we are a fairly normal, monogamous couple.

His equanimity with all of this impresses me. I think he handles it all very well, I must say better than

I would. I'm not sure I could be as supportive and understanding if our roles were reversed, and knowing that only adds to my admiration and respect for him.

I realize that I am an extremely fortunate woman, to be able to help others to find love and intimacy in their lives; to be in service in that way, and also to be able to have a love of my own, someone to hold me, to care for me, to listen and share my life; someone who lets me know that although I'm what I would call a fringe dweller, dancing outside the boundaries of polite society.. I belong. That belonging is one of the most important things in my life and I give thanks to my husband for that gift.

CHAPTER 6

JAMES

I looked down at James upside down face, as he lay between my legs with his head on a pillow, resting on my belly. His eyelashes rested softly on his cheeks, but the furrow between his eyebrows gave away a certain amount of tension. The first few buttons of his blue shirt were undone to expose his neck and a small tuft of light brown chest hair. We were about to begin the next exercise; facial caresses.

I had explained how we would do the exercise; much the same as hands and arms, only perhaps more gently, and he lay anticipating the first touch. As adults, we seldom have our faces touched except by lovers, and if we've never had one, it's yet another step into the unknown.

He had seemed a little less nervous when he arrived a half an hour earlier for our second session, smiling a little more easily and stepping forward voluntarily for a hug. In our update on the couch (which we would do in each session), he had told me that he was glad that he had decided to do this and that he thought it would make big changes for him in his life.

"Yes," I said, "and probably in more ways, good ways, than either of us can see right now."

He had done his homework, sensate focus exercises on his own body and said, of course, that he had never experienced his body that way before, really paying attention to how his body felt to him. Like many of us, most touching of his own body had been the simple, everyday functions of shaving, washing and so on.

"How about masturbation? Do you ever take your time with that?" I asked him. He blushed a little and admitted that any sensual touching was generally simply a rush to orgasm, without much focused awareness.

"Well, I know you're not alone in that," I told him. "But having this focusing skill will really help you to enjoy all the moments preceding orgasm and not just the orgasm. It'll get you back into your body when you become nervous in intimate moments and in fact, breathing and paying attention to sensation can help you to be calm in any anxious situation."

He nodded and smiled. "Okay, that sounds good."

Then we caught up on his week, what he'd been doing, how he had been feeling in general. "I guess I've been feeling a little different this week. I don't know exactly how, maybe a little excited or something? Like maybe things can change? I realized I've been noticing women a little bit more too."

I was really glad to hear him say so. We were very early in our work and his opening to the possibility of a different life was already beginning. It was good news for our work together: I've found that when a client has given up any idea of having what they want, they often shut down their awareness to that thing. In this case, women. It's just too uncomfortable and painful to look at women and couples every day, longing for that closeness and thinking you will never have it.

"Great, James, that's terrific!" I encouraged. "You know, you really began the change when you had the courage to enter this therapy." I waited a few moments to let that sink in and then asked, "So, shall we move ahead? I think you're ready for the next step, but before we do that I'd like to do some spooning and cuddling, if that's okay with you?"

He looked at me quizzically, "Spooning?"

"Yeah, where you're laying together, one in back of the other? You'll see. You know what it is, but maybe you just don't know the term. Can you help me move the coffee table and put the futon down?"

Once we had that done and the pillows were plumped up, I lay on my side and invited him to either lie in back of me to cuddle me or in front to be cuddled. He chose the back and we lay together, his knees touching the back of mine, his arm around me, with a hand that didn't know where to go, so I entwined his fingers in mine and held his hand against my diaphragm.

"James, I'd like you to pay attention to my breathing." We were still for a moment. "Now yours. Deep breaths in and out. I felt him relax a bit.

"Now I'm going to harmonize my breath with yours, so that we breathe at the same time." I held my breath for a moment, until I felt the end of his inhale and exhaled with him to synchronize our breathing. This is a very good exercise for relaxing and connecting with your partner and is actually very comforting.

We could have done the opposite, me inhaling, as he exhaled, which would allow our energies to connect and flow back and forth. However, I have found that this approach is more stimulating and I was seeking calm for him, so I opted for the harmonizing breath.

We breathed quietly for a while with me harmonizing with him and then switched roles so that he could have the experience of doing the harmonizing, as well. We continued until I felt the caution in the arm around me release, which allowed it to rest on my ribcage. We chatted easily for a bit about what we'd both been doing that week, and just hung out together, normalizing the experience of closeness.

After a bit, I asked "Are you feeling comfortable enough to begin our exercise for the day?" and his agreement brought us to the moment of his lying face up, head on the pillow between my legs.

I reminded him to breathe and to try to let go and just enjoy doing nothing. A face caress, while done with the same intention as doing arms or any other part of the body, feels slightly different to me than other caresses. As the passive partner I may be sensitive about my face. Depending on my state of mind, I may feel quite vulnerable. But, it can also be nurturing, soothing or may have sensual undertones.

When I am the active partner, it can feel quite intimate and at the same time my mind is in watchfulness, or overseeing, to ensure that I don't pull the skin or touch the eye too assertively. I keep my eyes closed most of the time, doing a check now and then to see where I am, but try to remain as much as possible in the realm of experiencing sensation.

"So, how're you doing, James? Ready to start?" I asked quietly.

He answered with a quiet "Uh huh."

"What I'd like to do is touch your face, ears, neck and a portion of your chest. Are you comfortable with all that?" He nodded in assent.

"Okay, then I'd like you to give me a boundary; how far down your chest do you think you'll be comfortable with me touching, inside your shirt?"

"Oh it's okay, anywhere is fine." His attempt to appear cool, I suspected.

"I'd like you to set the boundary. It's part of our establishing trust with each other and also, practicing it lets you know you can make reasonable boundaries. That will give you a sense of safety, of taking care of yourself. So, what do you think would be reasonable for you right now, if you're being honest with yourself?"

"Okay, well down to here," indicating the top of his rib cage.

"Okay. Anything you want to ask or say before we start?" I waited a moment for him to consider.

"I don't think so."

"Alright then. Now just close your eyes and try to enjoy, okay?"

A moment to breathe and I began by softly running the palm of one hand across his forehead, slightly dry to the touch, both hands down his cheeks, rasping over a mid-day stubble, to meet at his chin and examine the small cleft indented there, down the neck and across his sharply rising Adam's apple.

I retraced my steps, drawing my forearms back along his cheeks. I ran my fingers through the hair at the top of his forehead, brushing it against my hand

and arm, and dribbled my fingers down to his ears. His earlobes were spongy and velvety.

My fingertips found their way to the hard bone of his brow and traced the hairs marking his eyebrows, all lying down neatly. I ran my finger along his feathery eyelashes and circled around his cheekbones. Slowly, slowly and carefully feeling my way, I skimmed down the bridge of his nose to explore the flare of his nostrils.

I was interested in his lips. Would they be tightly sealed or softly relaxed? My fingers drew the delicate outline of his upper lip, corner to corner and along the bottom. Reaching the corner again, my index finger glided back along the soft plumpness of his lips themselves, to the other corner. His lips were closed, but not tightly.

Both hands, palms lightly connecting with his skin, skated smoothly down his neck and into the opening of his shirt to the surprise of warmth and softly curling hair. His skin felt firm and resilient, and his pectorals nicely defined. I kept my exploration to the top of his chest where I detected goose bumps as I smoothed my palms across his skin.

I felt his breath quickening and brought my hands back up to the surface to explore his face some more. My own feeling had become more sensual and I felt my movements reflecting my feelings. I held his head in my forearms for a moment and then swirled my hands from one side of his face to the other, all slowly, to get the most sensation I could from the contact between my skin and his.

I continued on for twenty minutes or so, always seeking sensation, both physical and emotional and finally placed my hands on his shoulders to let him know I had finished, and waited for his eyes to open.

James laid there for a couple of minutes with his eyes shut until I finally spoke softly. "So, how are you doing, James? Are you ready to talk for a minute?" He opened his eyes, but didn't speak for a moment or two, as if trying to determine exactly how he felt.

"It was nice," he said finally.

"What felt nice about it? What did you like the most?" I wanted him to be able to articulate with words of feeling and sensation.

"Well, I..I don't know how to describe it. It felt strange at first. I didn't know what to expect…this is all new to me." He fumbled a bit for words.

"Maybe you could use sensation words to talk about it? Like, soft or smooth or warm?"

"Yeah, it was all those things, after awhile. I couldn't relax very much in the beginning, but then when I started to, I could feel more. I guess I liked it the most when you touched my chest. Your hands were warm and kind of, I don't know, tingled or something." He then ran a finger over his own lips as if thinking about how my touch felt. "When you touched my lips it was kind of weird at first, and made me kind of nervous. It felt kind of personal, but after awhile I started to relax and it was okay. I kind of liked it. So what happens now?"

"Well, it's your turn to caress my face, so let's switch positions. Are you ready to do that? Or would you like to cuddle some more first?"

"No, I guess I'm ready...I'd like to do it. I'm kind of worried about touching your face too hard, though." He sat up and got out from between my legs.

He leaned back against the big pillows with his own legs open and clutched the small pillow to his abdomen. "Is this okay?"

"Let's see." I got between his legs and lay back with my head on the pillow. "Yes, I think this will be fine as long as you can reach my chest without stretching too much."

I shifted slightly to settle myself. "Okay, my boundary on my chest is here," I said, pointing to the edge of the top edge of my camisole. My breasts swelled slightly above it and I wondered how he might react to that; nicely stimulating or maybe too much?

I reminded James to take a deep breath into his belly and bring his attention to focusing on the sensations he received with his touch. I closed my own eyes and waited for a few moments and felt James' tentative, trembling fingers touching my forehead. They walked their way down my face, fingertips only, pressing here and there.

His nerves were apparent, but we had time; familiarity would ease his discomfort. As he went along, his touch became more confident and explorative, seeking new places to experience. He continued, still mostly with his fingertips, but became a little freer with the passing minutes.

I always anticipate and wonder how a client will do when it comes to touching my lips. Will he or won't he. There always seems to be a bit of nervousness or apprehension at first about doing that, as if it seems too personal or intrusive. Some clients can't do it for several tries, an indication to me of their discomfort with taking a chance in intimacy, an issue that may have to be addressed slowly.

James' index fingers played at the corners of my mouth and moved on, down my throat and onto my chest, back up to my shoulders and down again, to carefully and inquisitively touch the edge of my camisole. I could feel the upper curve of my breast pushing against his fingers and then he was gone again. He touched my ears and hair and went directly back to my lips again and drew one finger across from corner to corner as I had.

All in all, I felt that he was doing well at staying in touch with the sensations he was experi-encing. I could tell by the energy of his touch that he wasn't going away, into his head or losing focus too much. Consequently, I was fairly confident that we would be able to move on in the next session, depending of course, on how he felt about himself doing the exercise.

He finally finished and touched my shoulders lightly and said, "Okay, how was that for you?" in a very direct, slightly jarring voice.

Finesse, after all, does take some time to learn. The beginning and ending of an exercise, is as important as what happens in the middle. I like to think of it as gliding into the partner's field of energy and withdrawing as if that field was taffy and using that same attitude with my voice. It's a love touch, a love voice.

We talked about how I felt during it and how he felt about the process, as well as what it felt like to him. "Fine," was his quick and not very informative answer.

I smiled. "James, while I'm glad that the experience seemed to be okay for you, it doesn't tell me very much, so, if you don't mind, let's agree, for our work together, that 'fine' doesn't say enough. Words that really describe are best because I want you to be able to communicate with me: How you felt, what you felt, how you're feeling about yourself or about us. The most important part of any relationship is communication and we need to start at the beginning getting used to talking to each other in deeper ways."

He thought about that for a moment and nodded slightly. "Okay, I'll give it a try. Well, it felt really different than when we did arms. I was afraid that I'd hurt your face, so I tried to be careful, but it felt good to be touching you. The skin on your face feels different than your arms…maybe smoother and no hairs. It's kind of hard to feel and be careful at the same time." He paused. "How do you think I did?"

"For your first time caressing faces I thought you did well. I didn't feel you go into your head too much. Does that sound right, or do you feel like you *were* thinking a lot?"

"I did sometimes, but I tried to come back and pay attention to what I was doing as soon as I realized I was drifting or getting worried. I think mostly I was there with you."

"Me too," I nodded. "Now, I'd like to cuddle a little again, if that's okay." I lay down and James curled willingly around me. This time I could feel his energy wrapping warmly around me as well.

A short while later, after James left, I was sitting and making my notes on our second session, and feeling pleased with the both of us. It felt to me so far, that James was really going to make good progress with his issues and on top of that, I found him enjoyable to be with.

He seemed to understand the nature of the work we were doing; that it isn't really about sex. That's the easiest part. It's about his relationship with himself primarily, and with me and ultimately with the partner or partners of his choice. It was early yet in our work, but I felt that my report to Dr Johnston would have optimistic overtones.

CHAPTER 7
THE THERAPIST ROLE

One of my clients once said to me that he thought that everyone in talk therapy should be in surrogate therapy as well. Of course that isn't true, but his remark referred to the fact that in this kind of therapy, issues come bounding to the front more rapidly than in traditional therapy. Intimacy is a great instigator of emotion and emotion can speed us to the core of the work that needs to be done and a good therapist is invaluable to the process.

He or she is an integral part of this work and the beginning point for anyone seeking surrogate therapy. The client is usually seen by the therapist for several sessions before any referral is made. This gives the therapist the opportunity to assess the client's appropriateness for surrogate referral, as well as to determine the safety of the surrogate partner with the client, because surrogates often see their clients in their homes or other private offices.

Once the client has been referred, and is seeing the surrogate partner, he or she will also see the therapist after each session. Meanwhile, the surrogate will have reported to the therapist on her or his session with the client, disclosing any discussions that arose in check in, any particular insights and also a description of any intimate work done and anything that may have arisen out of that.

I make my reports to supervising therapists after each session and I relay what the client and I have done in that meeting, from our conversations to the physical exercises.

Conversations with a client include what's been going on in their world, as well as how they are feeling about the work itself and in general, how their spirits are and why. Anything pertaining to social interactions, attractions or lack thereof are talked about. As we go along, more and more discoveries are made about their family of origin and the real dynamics that existed in those first intimate relationships, much of which is often the reason for the client seeking therapy.

In the process of the therapeutic triad relationship, the therapist assists the client with any anxieties or emotional issues that may arise during the surrogate therapy sessions.

In addition the therapist may also be dealing with broader ranging issues in the clients life, which can be very relevant and are interwoven with the clients presenting difficulty. Issues that bring one to the surrogates' care often are reflected in their day-to-day life as well.

Clients usually experience apprehension as they begin surrogate therapy and often anxiety, when they begin to experience changes. Although some surrogates do have degrees in psychology, and others are generally psychologically astute and well equipped to give insights, the job of the surrogate is to do the intimate work that will give the client a sexual and relational foundation while the team therapist assists the client with the psychological issues and provides support for both the client and the surrogate.

The well being and healing of the client is always at the forefront of all our engagements with one another and he or she is always made aware that what one knows we all know, and that the therapist and I will be discussing their case in some detail.

In our reporting, the therapist and I bounce ideas and reflections off one another, give each other feedback and rely upon one another for information regarding where the client is in the process. Sometimes boundaries can become unclear between surrogates and clients and the therapist provides a steadying voice.

A therapist accustomed to working in the surrogate therapy triad is extremely valuable, but surrogates sometimes work with psychologists that are new to this modality and in that case the surrogate is educating the therapist as they go along. Also, some therapists might not be quite as comfortable talking about the sexual aspects of the case, if they have not had much experience working with clients with sexual, as well as emotional problems.

As work progresses, reports and discussions may need to be frank and graphic. The surrogate, with their attitude of comfort and naturalness around sexuality, has no problem talking about it, but it might take some getting used to for a therapist unaccustomed to it.

Many of the people I see are what we might call "touch deprived" since birth; not enough nurturing or hugs and cuddles growing up. Some are "grow yourself up kids," as one therapist puts it, sort of left on their own emotionally and not given much support or recognition. Overcoming religious sexual suppression is also often a factor in our work.

Reporting sensual physical exercises to the therapist is also important. I report as much in detail as is needed to let them know of any problems, challenges or successes and their feedback on a problem is often very helpful. I talk about my feeling about the client; what I think is happening and where I think he or she is, mentally and emotionally. If I am having an emotional problem myself with the client, the therapist is a sounding board and counselor for me as well.

The therapist relies upon my reports to plan his session with the client. Sometimes they will talk only about the sessions and sometimes more about their life in general as well.

It is his or her job to help me keep the client and myself on track and to watch for any signs of problems that might develop. Even though it is established at the beginning of therapy that open and honest communication must exist between the three of us, the client will sometimes tell the therapist things they would find difficult to tell me, or tell me things they are uncomfortable discussing with the therapist, although as our relationship deepens, that happens less and less frequently. It is also true that there are things that the client can tolerate hearing from me better than the therapist, and vice versa, of course.

Sometimes the therapist will give me suggestions about what we could do in the next session, but for the most part, most of them let me use my instincts and training to do my work. After all, they're not there in the session and things that happen usually do out of the substance of the relationship and the elements inherent in the moment.

I appreciate a therapist that is really involved with the internal process of the client and not interested in just sticking on a band-aid. In my view, because of the different psychological and emotional reasons for this person to be seeking help, various modes of therapy are required. Real healing requires self-discovery and behavioral changes, courage, determination, human affection and caring, self- awareness, sensual skills and the building of confidence.

In the 1970s there were surrogates who have now become therapists themselves, who are wonderful to work with, and of course some sexologists and traditional psychologists as well, but many conventional therapists these days don't know that surrogate therapy even exists, or may not be sure of the legality.

I hope I have impressed upon the reader and anyone seeking help in the sexual, relational area how important and critical therapists are to this process. Apart from the clinical observations, insights and support they provide, they also mark the difference between Professional Surrogate Therapy, that includes training and certification and follows the triad model, and others working on their own, misusing the title "surrogate."

The more therapists that work with us, the more healing occurs and I believe I can speak for all of us in professional surrogacy, when I say that we welcome the opportunity to work with and educate therapists unfamiliar with our work.

CHAPTER 8

JAMES

I n our last session, I had told James that at this point we had a choice of options for our present session. If he felt comfortable with moving on, we could go upstairs and get undressed to do mirror work, a process where we each face ourselves in the mirror and talk about how we feel about our bodies. If he didn't feel ready for that, we could continue on as we were, doing sensate caresses on the feet and legs.

I also had told him that I was pleased with his ability to stay focused and present in the exercises, so it became mostly a matter of his own emotional state and what he felt he could do. He had said he would think about it and let me know in this session.

Because I know how I feel each time I arrive at this point with a client, I am always deeply appreciative of the courage it takes for them to come here, let alone choose to take off their clothes with an almost stranger, not in a moment of passion but in the vulnerable process of facing themselves in the mirror.

Within the therapeutic model, each surrogate works according to his or her own sense of timing. Some take longer in the beginning than I might, working with dating and social skills first. I need for myself, to establish a relationship with someone before moving into deeper intimacy and more sensual or erotic work. However, I believe that for the client, getting into the sensual work gives them the confidence that they know what to do sexually, which in turn, gives them the freedom to actually go out, create dates and experience relationships.

For myself, and my clients, the dating issues and how to go about meeting potential partners is something we work on as we go along.

James had given it some thought during the week and had decided that he was comfortable with progressing to the mirror work, so now he and I were upstairs.

We had climbed my beige-carpeted stairs, myself in the lead with him following uncertainly behind and my big orange cat taking up the rear. A faint scent of incense had pulled us into a golden, sand colored room; my guest/work room.

A low bed holds the center of the room and although it is normally covered with a green and gold comforter, when I work with a client the comforter is removed, a green striped fitted sheet put down and a soft cream blanket laid at the foot for warmth and coziness. The room temperature, while a little overly warm when we step in, is comfortable for nakedness.

The large window to the side of the bed is covered with soft green and sheer cream curtains. There is a wrought iron mirror over the bed reflecting the closet doors on the opposite side of the room and a portable full-length mirror, which I'd placed earlier, in anticipation of this session, leaning against a bookcase in a corner.

My altar, a low wooden table partly covered by an embroidered white cloth, graces the room beneath a large Susan Seddon-Boulet print of a beautiful goddess, given to me by a friend. A stone head of the Amitaba Buddha sits in front of a sculpture of open, uplifted hands that hold beads and is draped with a small, sheer white scarf, a spiritual gift.

Here and there are meditation crystals and objects given to me by spiritual teachers and to one side, given to me by a woman friend that knows me well, is a hand sized, white piece of coral with a large half clam shell embedded in it. Sitting in the shell is a naturally shaped coral penis and balls. On the other side of the table is a small bronze statue of the Hindu god Shiva and his consort, wrapped in each others arms, her legs around his waist.

These are all my talismans, the things that carry energy for me; that remind me of who I am, my life and my explorations. The energy, the essence of the room is one of calm and clarity and for me, a perfect place to deepen the process of intimacy.

I know that for a client on his first entrance, the bed looms larger than life and definitely has an "Eek! moment of truth" factor to it. James stood awkwardly at the foot of it, looking as though he was trying to pretend it wasn't there, so I invited him to sit down on the end while I explained what we were going to do.

"Okay, so what we're going to do now is get our clothes off as quickly as possible and I have a way that will help us to get used to being naked together. We'll stand with our backs to each other and take everything off and when we're ready, I'll ask you to turn around and look at my back from the top of my head, to my feet. You don't need to say anything unless you have a question and when you're done, you'll turn around and it's my turn to look at you."

James nodded, looking a little dubious. "Okay."

"When I'm done we'll face each other and repeat the process together, all right? Make sure you look at all of me and don't skip anything, breasts, genitals, just treat it all the same. Sometimes you might get shy and want to skip over certain parts quickly, but it's important not to. Again, if you have questions, please ask, but otherwise, you don't need to say anything. Alright? Ready?"

He looked at me and I could see he was a little stunned or confused, so I continued. "There's a reason for doing it this way, James. It's so that we sort of get it out of the way and we won't have to do those sideways, secret glances at each other's bodies. You know the kind," and I gave him one, out of the corner of my eyes. "It really is okay, just to look at each other."

He gave a small laugh and nodded understanding, so I went on. "Once we've done that, we'll each take a turn in front of the mirror but don't worry, I'll start. Are you okay with that?"

He was chewing his lip and looked at me wide eyed. "Sure, okay."

I went on. "I'll talk about my body from head to toe, talking about how I feel about each of my parts, the ones I like and parts that I'm not happy with. I'll talk about how I think things look, how they feel and how they work. I'm going to let you know everything I feel about my body. That way it's all out in the open and there's no need for me to try to hide my unacceptable parts and wonder if you see them that way too. No comments are necessary, no trying to make something okay for me, alright? You just witness. Then when I'm done, it's your turn. Does that feel doable for you?"

"I guess so." He looked apprehensive, of course and I felt a little nervous myself.

I took his hand. "You know, I want you to know that I'm nervous too. Maybe not as much as you, because I've done this lots of times, but even so, it's never easy to present myself to someone new. I have all kind of feelings about my own body and it feels very vulnerable." I smiled, "Just to let you know you're not alone, okay?'

He nodded, "Okay, but I can't believe you're nervous."

"Yeah? Well I'm only human, too." I gave a small shrug and smiled. "So, anyway let's get started."

We stood up and I pointed James toward a wall that has no view of any of the mirrors on the sides of it, so that he couldn't see me from the side as I got undressed. It's my own little quirk. Being watched at this stage feels like I'm being spied upon and whether the client has that intention or he even notices the mirror or not is not the issue, it's all about me and my feeling vulnerable before I'm ready to be so.

I turned my back to him and took off all my clothes. Behind me, I could hear him doing the same. I always try to not take glimpses of my clients in the process either, affording them the same time to prepare that I need. It seems kind of odd to me sometimes that I'm so protective of these few moments. After all, in a few of them it's all going to be out there for inspection.

"Ready?" I asked when I was prepared to start.

"I guess so, ready as I'll ever be," he replied uncertainly.

"Okay, so turn around and look at me and don't skip anything. Give yourself time to get comfortable looking and try to really see me."

This is for me personally, the most vulnerable moment. There's something about having someone behind you where you can't see their face or read their expressions that feels really uncomfortable; even more so, than when they're in front of you, where the most sacrosanct parts are being seen. I can always feel my hands at the ends of my wrists that don't know what do with themselves. They always want to hold each other in front of me.

I feel shy and I'm so, so conscious of my hips and I feel myself shifting from foot to foot and I have to remind myself of where I am and what I'm doing, bringing back into consciousness that other part of me that can handle this. The one that is wise, that knows that this feeling will pass momentarily. This time was no different in that respect, for me. I experienced all my little discomforts and managed to bring myself into balance by the time James said he was done with his inspection.

"Any questions?" I asked.

"Uh, no, I don't think so. So, shall I turn around?"

"Yep, my turn." We both turned around and I began to survey the landscape, the length of his body from the back. Reasonably broad shoulders with a little slump, moderate build, not much hair on his back, just a tiny little patch at the waist-line, small love handles, a fairly hairless round butt and quite strong and well shaped legs. I took a minute or so doing it as he stood as still as a statue.

I finished and cleared my throat quietly. "Okay, I'm done. No questions on my part either, so can you turn around now?"

He hung his head shyly as he turned but looked up finally, to face me. I reminded him again to look at everything from head to toe and to take the time to have a visual experience of my body as I would his. His body was nice enough, a very little bit of a belly, and healthy in appearance. His penis was reacting, I suspected, to his nervousness, and was shyly shrinking back into his body; a normal reaction to the situation to be sure.

I felt much more comfortable with his gaze as I faced him than I had been before and I waited until he indicated that he felt complete. Then I directed him to sit on the bed again to watch while I looked into the full-length mirror I had set up in the corner.

"Your job, James, is just to witness my observations about my body. There's no need for comment, or to try to fix my feelings or give a different perspective. Just watch, alright?"

With his assenting nod, I began the grocery list of my body; my face that was never pretty enough for me, my shoulders that are not wide enough, my breasts that I do love, full and pink-nippled as they are, a delicate waist and a belly and hips that are womanly, but reflect some of the extra ten pounds I carry.

I talked about my pussy and how I used to think it weird looking, but how I had come finally to appreciate it's beauty as the result of workshops I'd done where I saw other women's sacred parts. My dancers legs were shapely and strong and my flat feet were starting to give me trouble.

There are things I love about my body and many things that I would change if I could, but as I reflected upon the figure in the mirror, the overall effect and appearance was one of wholesome sensuality and basically pleasing to my eye, which I said.

Then it became James turn. He stood up and faced the mirror and eyed himself, running his hand through his brown hair, surveying his face by turning his head left and right trying to get a profile angle. He said he liked the color of his hair and didn't mind the bit of gray and was grateful that he still had quite a lot of it, unlike his father, who had developed the Friar Tuck hairdo at James age. He thought his face fairly good looking. At least he'd been told so by some people.

He seemed reasonably secure with his body, even though he felt he needed to be more motivated with his gym visits. He said he didn't know about his penis, that he'd always felt that maybe it was a little on the small side and it certainly wasn't reliable.

He surveyed it grimly and put his hand protectively over it for a moment as if afraid of my agreement. At the moment, under scrutiny, it had probably become as small as it could get and actually looked fairly average to me. A penis can never be judged, if one is inclined to do so, in it's flaccid state. In full erection the smallest looking limp penis can take on surprising proportions.

At any rate, I simply raised my eyebrows, and said "Huh!" and James continued on expressing satisfaction with his legs and feet and finished by saying "Well, I guess that's about it."

He turned to face me and I patted the bed, inviting him to come and lie down next to me, which he seemed grateful to do. Anything to avoid scrutiny at the moment, I imagined.

I turned to face him as he laid down face up and placed his hands across his chest.

"Well, how was that? Excruciating or not too bad?"

"Not too bad, but it sure felt weird talking about myself like that. I mean, whoever does that? I guess I think all those things, but saying them out loud is kind of hard."

"Yes, I know, for me too, even though I've done it lots of times. But now it feels pretty easy to be with you naked. How about you?"

He nodded agreement. "Yeah, definitely less intimidating, but I'm still nervous."

"Well, yes, that's totally understandable," I assured him. "So now, I'd like to cuddle for a minute before we begin our next sensate exercise. Just to relax and get used to one another for a few minutes. I'll cuddle you this time, if that's alright?"

"Okay," he said, turning over on his side with his back to me. I curled up around him, putting my arm across him and resting my head against the back of his shoulder. His back was warm and I could feel the hair on his legs, where they touched mine. I was conscious of my breasts nestled against his back and my pelvis that was resting against the top of his buttocks.

He smelled freshly washed and lightly scented with a crisp aftershave or cologne. He held my hand where it folded across his belly and we fell comfortably still for a few minutes breathing together and soaking up each other's energy.

After awhile I asked him if he felt comfortable and ready to begin our sensate pleasuring. Taking turns as usual, we were now going to do back caresses, which involves touching backs, buttocks, legs, everything, without any specific focus on any one part. Just touching the other for our own self-pleasure.

He made himself comfortable on his belly in the middle of the bed while I found some music on the CD player in the nightstand and put it on. I climbed back onto the bed and sat for a moment next to him and asked if he needed a pillow under his stomach, which he turned down. I reminded him that arousal was okay if it happened and okay if it didn't, that we wouldn't be doing anything with it anyway, but that if he needed at any time to adjust himself for erection comfort that would be fine.

Non-demand caresses are wonderful in that there's nothing you need to do, no expectations, no goals, just pleasure for both partners.

Once a client and I get to full body caresses, any nervousness I'm experiencing generally leaves and I'm focused on the enjoyment and hoping to take my client in with me.

I began by placing my hands on his back, getting him used to my touch. As I felt him relax, I began my exploration of his body, using my hands and arms at first, feeling the texture and warmth, the soft down on his back and buttocks.

After awhile, as I got more into what I was doing, I began changing my own position, sitting, leaning, stretching out, my hips, my arms sometimes brushing his body, my face purposefully brushing his back. I leaned over him to put my face in the crook between his head and shoulder, to breathe his scent. My breasts brushed his body and my legs felt long next to his.

I explored the little valleys between his ribs and cupped the roundness of his butt with the inside of my elbow. I brushed down the outside of his legs to press the arches of his feet and came back tracing the inside of his thighs, to the space between where I swept up alongside, but not touching, the soft sack of his balls that sat like a puddle on the bed.

Along with all the sensations of my body, were sensations of emotion. With tenderness and caring, came a sense of my own power, my sensuality, my love of connecting in this way, skin to skin, but all wrapped up with those feelings was also an awareness of the need to be careful, to not push the envelope too fast.

This was all new to my partner and while it was important for me to let myself go enough to allow him to see the possibilities for pleasure, I couldn't make assumptions about his emotional state and I didn't want to overwhelm him. That would certainly have defeated the purpose, which I would define as erotic ease.

After fifteen minutes I brought my hands to stillness between his shoulder blades, over his heart center, and sat for a few moments, not only to let him know I had completed, but to reconnect in a quiet way and leave his energy gently. Then I laid down facing him and waited for him to emerge from wherever he was.

James turned his head, opened his eyes and gazed at me, saying nothing. His eyes were soft and kind of questioning, maybe already jumping to "what am I supposed to do now?" or "what's next?"

I can never predict a partner's reaction at this point. Sometimes I myself have had a wonderful time and their response to my question as to what they felt or what they experienced gets a "Nice" or "Good," which usually prompts an inner sigh on my part. While my ego of course, would prefer an answer of "amazing," I need to hear what was real for them, so I always press for descriptions of physical sensation, or emotions or tension levels. In James case, he said that he was surprised that he felt relaxed most of the time and even sometimes felt a little aroused.

"Can you tell me what you liked best?" I prompted him.

"Well, I liked all of it, but I really liked it when you sort of leaned across me and I felt your breasts brushing me. That felt great and I think I started to get a hard on, but I felt a little nervous about that, like I wasn't sure it was okay. I know you said before that it was okay if I did or didn't but, I don't know, it just felt a little strange. But good! I also liked it when you put your face next to mine. It felt sexy, but then I worried if my breath was okay. Was it okay?" This all came tumbling out in a rush of embarrassment.

"Yes, it seemed fine. At least I didn't notice anything. I could just smell your hair and your cologne or aftershave. It smells nice."

"Good, I always worry about that kind of thing, but you know what? Doing all this makes me think that maybe I didn't spend enough time like this in the past, those other times. Have you done this all the time in your own relationships?"

I thought about it for a minute and said, "Probably not enough, but I have it when I want to do it. Sometimes it's fun to just have a hot quickie. What we're doing with all this is giving you some tools and also some confidence that you know what to do, and have skills that you can rely on. Just knowing that will give your body permission to have erections, and those occasional times when it's not cooperating, well, you can still play, please your partner and give yourself space to become aroused."

I took a moment to stretch my arms a bit. "Anyway, let's get back to the moment and cuddle for a minute and then it's your turn, okay?"

"Yeah, I'm a little nervous but, yeah." He wrapped around me and we snuggled for a few minutes until we were comfortable enough to start and he sat up cross-legged on the bed beside me. I suspected that he was, like most men I know, fairly tight in the hips, so the sitting position is not a necessarily a good one for this experience.

"Can I show you how I move when I do it, so that I have the use of both hands and arms?" I sat up and demonstrated how I move from position to position, to reach all parts of the body and to be able to use my own body as a kind of dance. I kneeled, hunkered down with my butt in the air, laid on my stomach, my side, any way that felt comfortable and gave me access.

James watched me with a frown but said he'd give it a try, so I made myself comfortable with a pillow under my belly to ease my back, sighed and surrendered to the bed in anticipation of being touched.

The tension in the hand James placed on my back reminded me to tell him to take a breath and try to relax a little before he started. I knew that his performance anxiety was beginning to express its self, so I also reminded him that this experience was for his pleasure, not mine, although I would reap the benefits as well. When a partner is truly enjoying touching one's body, there is definitely a sense of deliciousness transmitted to the touch-ee, the source of their pleasure. It's a circle.

After a few moments I felt his hand on my back again, softer this time, making a few scouting passes up and down my back. I knew it would take a bit for him to settle into the exercise, but he began brushing my body with his hand, down one leg and back up to my shoulder, down the other side of my body and back up, down my arms and back to the first side again.

After a minute or two, repetitive action had set in, a dead give away that he wasn't present, but in his head or out in the ethers. Then, all of a sudden his face pressed against my back. He rubbed it against me, moving around my back, quickly, almost roughly, thoughtlessly. It felt like a wrestling match between my back and his face.

"Whoa, James, slow down," I directed, stretching out the "slow." "You'll feel more if you go slowly."

At that, he sat back and did slow his action, but I could feel his tension. "See if you can feel my ribs, or the space between, or sense the muscles in my body. Don't massage me, just try to feel. The slower, the better. This is for you. Use the experience to get to know the terrain of my body."

He began again, moving slowly and, I felt, paying attention more closely. After awhile, I began to feel him connecting to my body, to me. After some time, he finally laid down beside me continuing to touch me.

"Okay," he said, his voice indicating that he'd made a discovery. "I like this, touching you this way. I think you're right. For me, going slower is much better. I think in the past I was so nervous that I moved too fast, but this feels good, this is what I like."

It's an important moment for James; just beginning to get the idea and starting to connect with what worked for him. That awareness of ourselves gives us a base, a place to connect with our body and our heart.

That same awareness gives us a safe place from which to break out and explore and to actually be in truly intimate relationship with another.

I turned over and reached out to give him a hug. "That's it, James. That's a great awareness for you and you know, once you began to enjoy yourself it felt wonderful to me. One of my clues about myself is that when I feel your connection, my own body wants to move, to respond, but I purposefully didn't allow that right now. I didn't want you to hook into giving me pleasure and having to perform. You need to focus in yourself for now. Later on, we'll have time for more response and it'll be fun, but right now the key is to stay with what pleasures you about my body, going slowly and really feeling what you touch. Until I see you again I want you to continue to work with this idea when you're touching things."

"You mean when I touch anything? I don't know if I have that kind of concentration," he asked frowning.

"No, not all the time of course, but you can specifically touch animals, fabrics, whatever appeals to you. Do it on yourself as well, being both the touch-er and the touch-ee, the doer and the receiver. See what your body feels like when you go slowly, as well as how it responds to touch. How do you like to be touched, what parts of your body are more sensitive? Touch your genitals the same way, without the goal being masturbation. Just to focus on sensation. In fact, even if it feels too good, no masturbation right then. Save it for later." I raised my eyebrow to drive the point home "It's not the focus, know what I mean?"

James grinned, a cute smile that showed his even, well cared for teeth. "Yeah, I know. I'll save it. It'll probably be tough, but whatever you say, coach," and with that, he gave me another hug. It had started to feel good between us, looser, more ourselves, a little at a time.

Finally, disengaging myself and sitting up I said, "Well, time for me to send you out into the cold, James. How do you feel?"

"I feel pretty good. I know I have quite a ways to go, but so far, it feels like I'm making some progress, so... good."

As we dressed, I told him that I would be making my report to our therapist and reminded him that in his session with Dr Johnston, if things came up after he left, to be sure to address those issues or questions with the doctor.

We scanned the room for any items of his and headed downstairs to say goodnight and as I saw him off I felt satisfied and content. It felt like it had been a good learning session for him and an excellent gateway session for the rest of our work together. It was a good start for James.

CHAPTER 9
JAMES

"So how has your week been James? Anything come up from our last session that you need to ask or talk about?" I questioned, as we sat on the couch the following week.

"No, not really. I enjoyed all the touching we did." He took a sip of water and continued.

"I guess I'll get better at it with more practice, but I was wondering how I would do with someone else, like the first time I'm with a woman I'm dating. I'm worried that I'll probably be nervous again," he admitted. "But I guess I don't have to worry about that right now anyway. I don't even know anyone I'd want to date."

"Yeah, I'd say you're jumping the gun a bit," I said with a nod and a smile. "We have a lot of things to cover that will give you more confidence. When that moment comes with someone new, of course you'll be nervous, everyone is. It's sort of built into the anticipation of being with someone you're attracted to. Some of us even find that kind of exciting."

James looked doubtful.

"It can be, you know. The trick is to be able to keep your balance and not let the nervousness stop you from trying new things, and you know what? Sometimes it helps to just say that you're nervous. That way it's out in the open and you're not trying to hide it. She may find it flattering and step up herself, to soothe you in the moment. Anyway as we go along, I think you'll find that you'll feel a little differently about it later and also, you'll get some idea of how to handle the situation, so not to worry right now, okay?" This bit of honest reassurance is always helpful in the early stages of the work.

"Yeah, I'm sure you're right. I feel like I have a lot to learn so, I'll try to just stick to the plan and see what happens."

"Good attitude. So, how did your session with Dr. Johnston go?"

"It was good. We just talked a little about you and me and spent more time talking about my family and stuff, mostly about my relationship with my mom, and how I could never do very much right with her. She was pretty critical, I guess. I never seemed to be able to please her, so she'd always be after me. Dr Johnston said that maybe that's part of the reason I get so nervous about dating; that I'm afraid of being criticized."

He had been sitting forward on the couch, his hands folded under his chin. Straightening, he fell back lightly into the cushions.

I turned my body more to face him. "Uh-huh, so then you get so nervous that you can't do anything," I said, agreeing with that assessment. "Also, constant criticism as a child can really affect how you feel about yourself in general, don't you think?"

"Yeah." He reached for his glass on the coffee table again and took several gulps of water. "Actually I think that I have trouble with fear of criticism in some other places in my life as well."

"Well, while you work on some of that childhood stuff with him, we'll work on giving you the tools that will give you some confidence. So I'd like to begin our work today with how you feel about making first contact with a date. You know, touching her or making physical contact for the first time, letting her know you're interested and attracted to her, physically. How do you think you would do with that?"

"Not very good. I'd be nervous from the beginning, so I'd feel kind of awkward or clumsy or something. I'd really be afraid that my inexperience would show."

"Well, obviously, it hasn't been completely debilitating in the past, because you have managed to be taken to the bedroom a couple of times. But let's see if we can find ways to make it more comfortable."

I asked him to show me how he might start to get close to me so, after giving it consideration for a minute, he shifted a little on the couch to get a little closer and reached out to put his hand on my hand and softly stroked it. Not too bad.

"How did that feel? Did it feel awkward to you?" he wanted to know.

"It felt a little stiff, but it's a good start and it will get better as you become more comfortable with it and find more ways to do it." I answered.

"You did fine and from now on, without any coaching from me, each time you come to our session, it's your assignment to make the first move to get closer, okay? It could be taking my hand, or physically moving closer, but something that feels relatively comfortable for you, and we'll talk about it as we go along. For now though, I'd like to continue with our sensate exercises. So, on that note, shall we go upstairs?"

"Okay, let's go," he said and got up from the couch, offering me his hand. A sweet, kind of old fashioned, gentlemanly gesture, it took me a bit by surprise, but in a very nice way. I took his hand and got up and we headed for the stairs and chatted easily as we made the ascent.

Before too long we would need to integrate the living room with the bedroom, making a sensual transition from couch to bed, but we definitely weren't there yet.

When we got to the guest room James began immediately taking off his clothes, which could have been either nervousness or excitement and anticipation, or more likely a combination of all of that. I went to the bathroom and when I got back he was on the bed under the cream colored blanket, with it tucked up neatly under his arms, which were plastered against his body. Okay, clearly it was nervousness.

I took off my own clothes, as matter-of-factly as I could, knowing that his brown eyes were watching me and I felt again that bit of shyness that comes with the consciousness of my own body. As I lifted the blanket and got into the bed, I became aware of the softness of my belly and breasts as they moved with me, drooping some and I quickly nestled up against James warm body, where I felt safe from my own judgment.

It has always been interesting to me how comfortable I am being touched, compared to how I feel when I'm being looked at. I do know that after someone has become familiar with touching my body, they usually come to like the way it looks as well, if they weren't turned on by me at first. I pulled the blanket up around my shoulders and James lifted his arm to let me rest my head on his shoulder, as I slid my arm across his belly and gave a little squeeze.

We lay there for a few minutes quietly and when I suggested that he spoon me, he turned on his side and gave me the arc of his body to curve into. As I did so, I felt the rubbery softness of his dick against my butt. Ah! The unreliable penis developing into a chubby, a good sign. More proof that relaxation is the key.

After we both felt comfortable and relaxed I suggested that we begin the next exercise. "Now I'd like to do some frontal body caresses, with no particular focus on erogenous zones," I explained. With some extremely anxious clients, we would do frontal body with no genital touching at all, until the client is emotionally ready for it, but I felt that James was. If it turned out that I was wrong, we would backup.

"So what that means is that I'm going to treat your penis the same way as your elbow. I won't ignore it, but I won't hang around trying to make it happy either." We both laughed at the idea of a happy penis. "Remember too, the same thing always applies; erections are okay, no erections are okay. Nothing is going to happen with it, so no cock watching, alright? You've been doing enough of that in your life. Just let yourself sink into receiving the pleasure that your skin gives you. Ready?"

He had turned over onto his back and as he closed his eyes he said, "I think so."

I began as I always do, taking a moment to drop into connection with myself and said lightly, "Okay, I'm going to touch you."

I put my hand on his heart center for a few moments to establish a connection with him and then began my exploration of sensation. I started slowly with my hands, getting used to touching, moving across his body, sensing the sparse, coarse hairs on his chest and around his navel, getting him accustomed to my touch as well.

Once we get to the front of the body, the vulnerability factor goes up for the receiver, of course, and the opportunity for "spectatoring," watching one's body reactions instead of feeling or being in them, is dramatically increased. This is often when emotional issues really begin to surface, when one is lying bare in another's hands. Performance anxiety, fear of judgment, fear of humiliation, of being rejected find fertile ground here.

I don't always know what a partner is feeling until afterwards, unless tension in their body reminds me to tell them to breathe or to relax, so I try to go about my work of seeking pleasure and let go of my own "watcher."

James' penis had returned to its relaxed state and it remained soft and nestled into the cleft between his thigh and his balls. I skimmed over it at first, along with the rest of his body and finally at some point, lifted it out of its comfort zone to explore it further, took it in my hand, feeling the density of it, traced around the mushroom shaped head and then moved on again. I continued my sensual adventure for about twenty minutes and I noticed that James still breathed easily as I finished and laid back down on my side facing him.

As we talked James admitted that he had to remind himself that it was okay not to have a hard on.

"I know you said it was always okay either way, but it just seemed like, because you were touching me and it felt nice, that something should've been happening. I mean that's what's happened before…nothing!"

I could feel his anxiety. "James, it's not unusual for this to happen. It's not supposed to lead to an erection. Sometimes it does anyway, but the more okay you are with nothing happening, except feeling good, the more space you give your body to respond naturally. Maybe you remember that old phrase 'a watched pot never boils?' Well, same thing here. You just have to give in to feeling sensation and pleasure."

I stroked his arm. "I'm not worried about this and I know you can get there too. You'll see, this does work."

"Okay, I guess 'cause this is all new to me, that might be what it is too. It's just hard not to think about it when it's been such a bummer in the past. I'm just always fighting, thinking that that's all there's ever gonna be. Sometimes it feels hopeless!"

"I understand that you feel that way, but you know, you don't really have a reason to think that. This is a situational thing. You don't have any trouble when you masturbate, right?"

James nodded his agreement. "Yeah, not usually."

"Alright, so we know it's not a functional problem. It's just a matter of getting your mind to relax and let go and have fun rather than performing."

I rose up on my elbow to look down into his face. "I believe you can and will be able to do that, James. You're really doing great so far. This is all new to you and I think you're handling it well."

There are a lot of these repetitive reminders that happen until a client has some affirming experiences that raise confidence in his body's ability to function.

"But, is it alright with you to let go of this for now and move on? Or do you need to talk more about it?" I asked.

Shrugging, with a little tilt of his head, he replied, "No, I guess not. It's not going to get any better just talking about it."

"No, but it *will* get better, you'll see. Now, it's my turn to receive and I'm ready for both of us to have some pleasure at your hands. What about you? Ready?"

"Okay, I guess so," he said, with some hesitation.

"Now, you concentrate on your pleasure and I'll concentrate on mine. Remember, the deal is, no particular attention to private parts. No probing or penetration, just touching. Okay?"

I turned over on my back, sighed and released into the bed, my arms out and my legs open enough to allow his touch. It might seem that this would be a vulnerable moment, but the truth is that I have never, in all my work, had a client that took advantage of this position. In fact, very often I have to lead them past their own shyness to touch me, by taking their hand and guiding it between my legs, sometimes with a little instruction to stroke or stop a moment to just feel the texture and softness of the outer labia.

James rolled toward me and sat up, adjusting himself to find a position, from which to begin. His hand on my diaphragm felt warm but a little damp.

"Would you like some powder, James?

"Yeah, I guess I'm nervous again."

"No problem, it's right there," I said, flicking my head in the direction of the speaker beside the bed, where I keep my surrogate accoutrements, condoms, lubricating gel, a small hand towel and powder.

He reached across me to get it and as he leaned in I could detect the faint scent of soap and the slight sharpness of testosterone and after a moment, the soft, fresh smell of the powder as I felt the dusty drops fall across my body.

His hand returned to my diaphragm and began its journey across the terrain of my body. He stayed to the middle and extremities first, moving somewhat quickly, but finally slowing down, with no reminder from me. Good.

He circled my breasts, cupping his hand around the fullness to the sides, slid down to probe my naval for a second and moved on down my legs, coming back up my inner thighs, but avoiding my genitals. Whenever a body part gets left out, I find that it seems to have an anticipation all its own, wanting to be touched like everything else, so although I could focus on his touch fairly well, my own watcher was engaged wanting to see if he would actually get there.

When he finally tentatively touched my nipples, it seemed to embolden him and on his next excursion down my body he brushed over my labia. He continued to include all my parts and actually stopped here and there to feel a muscle or the texture of my skin, but never did more with my genitals than brush them, so when he seemed like he'd finished, I took his hand, placed it between my legs and said, "I'd like you to just sort of press a little to really know what it feels like."

With my hand over his, I manipulated his fingers to press back and forth. After a few moments, I released his hand and asked him to explore on his own and he did so, pressing and stroking. He then spent another minute or so on the rest of my body again and when he stopped, I turned on my side to look at him.

"Well, how did that seem to you?"

"Good, I liked it and I think I did okay. I didn't think too much. I tried to just concentrate on how you felt. To me, I mean. I did wonder once if you thought I was doing okay, but mostly I really enjoyed it. I guess I wasn't sure about how I was supposed to touch your um, genitals, though, so it helped when you took my hand. How do you think I did?"

"Well, I enjoyed it too, I did wonder for a bit if you were going to get around to touching my yoni (a tantric word for pussy), but you did, so that was great. It didn't seem to me that you were in your head much and I can usually tell, from how you're touching me, whether you're in the moment or not. So, good, great, I think we're ready to move on. What do you think?"

"Yeah, I'm ready. I'm actually kind of surprised that I'm doing okay. I think it's easier if I'm the one touching than when you're touching me. When you touch me I think too much about my dick."

"I know. But that's not uncommon. It may have something to do with my being able to receive and just enjoying pleasure for pleasure's sake. But, that will get easier for you too, as we go along. And now, it's about time to get you on your way, my friend."

"So your assignment for next time is to do kegels and a sensate sensitivity exercise. Do you know what kegels are?"

James, frowning, shook his head no.

"It's the pubococcygeal, or pc muscle that you use to stop the flow of urine, if you need to stop before you have finished. You know, the one that can also make your hard on bounce a little?"

James nodded, looking a little embarrassed.

I continued "Exercising that muscle will allow you to use it, to control your ejaculation, provide firmer erections and also help prevent incontinence as you get older. On another level, I believe it charges the pelvis with energy, to be used not only for sex, but for living in general."

I sat cross-legged facing him and had him contract the muscle, to imagine that he was urinating and stopping the flow. I told him to do a series of both slow and fast contractions. His face took on a look of concentration that made a deep crease between his eyebrows as he focused on the contractions.

"Do you have it?" I couldn't help laughing a little at his facial contortions and my own laughter made him laugh as well. "You look like your having a hard time with it."

Still laughing, he said, "Yeah, I guess I am. Let me try again to see if I can do it. I'll try to imagine myself taking a leak. I know I've done this before, it's just when you think about it,… you know, it's different."

This time the look of concerted effort dissolved into one of satisfaction. "Okay! I think found it. Now how many do I have to do again? The slow ones are tough."

"I know, they keep wanting to slip away, hmm? They'll get stronger, so try to hold up to 10 slow counts and eventually it'll be pretty easy. Do ten slow and 30 fast contractions."

"I never heard of this. Is this something people do?"

"No," I laughed, "but they should. It would help us to not pee our pants when we get older. Sexually, the pc muscle can be interesting. Some women with strong pc's can kind of squeeze and milk a penis and for men, using them can help with holding back ejaculation or sometimes, with me for instance, bring on orgasm.

"So try to do a set at least once a day, twice if you think of it, so eventually you'll be able to do maybe a hundred. You can do it driving your car, or sitting at your desk, or whatever and no one will ever know. As long as you don't make that face anyway." I took his face in my hands. "For a nice looking guy it's not a great look!" I teased.

James reached up and took my hand in his. "Okay coach, what else?"

"The other thing I want you to do, is the sensate caress on your own body again, but this time really paying attention to the areas that have the most sensitivity, not only in feeling, but that also might stimulate erotic images or ideas. You know, that make you feel sexy or make you think about sex. Okay? I think that will be enough for you to do until next time."

"How many times should I do it?" he asked, as we rose and began dressing.

"This one I would do at least a couple of times and next time we meet, you'll have an idea of what you can show me as your erotic or erogenous zones.

Finally, fully clothed, we walked back down into the coolness of the living room, where I hugged him goodbye, let him out and removed my sign on the door that says, "Please do not disturb, counseling session in progress."

Another good session, with a sense of intimacy and ease growing between us that I knew had just begun, but I found myself wondering if and when any deeper material might surface. So far it had been pretty easy, textbook almost. But in the deep waters of sexuality, one never knows what might be lurking.

CHAPTER 10
EXERCISES AND GAMES

I have written about my sessions with James as though we were able to follow the surrogate model fairly closely. The purpose of this is to give the reader a clear idea of what the model is and how it works.

The actuality is that it could easily take longer, with more than one session spent at a particular level before we move on to the next, depending on the severity of the client's problem, encountered anxiety or discomfort. We might need to remain at a particular level for awhile before we move to the next. This can be due to a client having difficulty with some aspect of the work, or simply being in a place of resistance.

With touch deprived, or touch phobic clients, more time in the beginning needs to be spent in establishing comfort in that basic area. Sometimes it might be necessary to really ground a client in a particular skill or to help them really get a sense of what relaxation or focused attention is for them. Just learning to receive pleasure takes time in its own right.

Common hurdles include resistance, where the client is making steady progress but suddenly becomes frustrated when emotional issues or memories are triggered, or because their problem hasn't been "fixed" yet. And, of course, there are always going to be clients who have unrealistic expectations when things aren't working the way they think they should. Whether it takes one session or several, we generally get through it and move on.

Occasionally the client or myself are low on energy, so the session might take a more nurturing direction, with lots of touching and holding and talking. But whatever the form, I have seldom, if ever, had any session that was not worthwhile. The client and I together are creating and modeling a relationship, a good one that will work in their life: a relationship that is caring, supportive, honest, and has boundaries that honor the individuals and the relationship.

Also, the time spent in intimate sharing and talking, often leads to insights for both of us, into the nature of the client's relationship with their sexuality and the forces in their childhood that constructed it. This provides material for the triad therapist and the client in their sessions as well.

Breath and relaxation exercises are crucial, whatever the problem is. It aids the client in getting to a place of comfort, so that we can move into the intimate work and gives him a reliable way to relax when he experiences anxiety in the world. Homework in practicing relaxing breath is almost always the first assignment.

Trust exercises are necessary for some clients that have issues around trusting others. I may even blindfold clients and lead them around the house and yard. It seems basic, but it calls upon the client to let go and surrender, to put themselves in someone else's hands and trust that they will be safe.

We might also blindfold each other, one at a time, during sensual play, where the passive partner is required to release their own control, even though and sometimes especially because, it's pleasurable. We are built for pleasure, but sadly, most of us haven't been taught that.

At some point, with a client with no dating experience, we might take a walk to practice taking and holding hands or with arms around one another's waist, chatting and walking, just to practice getting comfortable with that kind of worldly interaction.

A client who has control issues, having to manage himself emotionally so carefully and completely that they are unable to function in relationship, could be helped by repeating the A-B game, where the partners sit opposite each other with their hands mid air, palms facing one another and barely touching. Partner A begins leading partner B in a hand dance, still barely touching, no holding on. The receiver, partner B, is to let go of control and let the other guide them. Then, without speaking, except for my calling the switch, the roles are reversed and Partner B leads.

Once the client is used to the idea and as we repeat the exercise over time, it becomes easier for them to relax and the movement can move faster and faster in the switching from A to B. This game helps the client to become aware of when they are trying to manage or control and how to relax and sink into the moment, something that can translate into being better able to let go and receive pleasure at the hands of another. It also teaches them to be sensitive to the energy between themselves and their partner.

Many clients have trouble asking for or acting on what they want, if they are even able to think or imagine anything they might want. At some point in our work, we might play the "May I, Will You" game, where we take turns asking for something from the other relevant to things we've already done together. We might say "May I stroke your face?" or he could say, "Will you touch my dick?" and so on, depending on where we are in the work. It's also an opportunity to hear the word "no" and be able to tolerate it and stay in relationship.

Either partner can comply with a request, or if not comfortable with it or doesn't feel like it, they are free to say "no" without explanation. It also requires one to be the person saying "no" sometimes, which doesn't come so easily either. There are moments when I say it that I feel a sense of chagrin. Moments when I feel that saying what I want to say, rather than just going along, will hurt my partner's feelings, so I benefit from these exercises, myself. Of course, the fun of the game is that there needs to be plenty of "yes's" as well; the rewards for asking reinforcing the process itself.

Even clients that don't have much difficulty asking are surprised at their reticence in saying no or tell me that it was hard to hear the word, even though they realize that it's an exercise.

With a client that is uncomfortable talking about sex frankly, discomfort using sexual words, or using talk during sex, we might make a game out of taking turns saying every slang word we can remember for different body parts and for the various kinds of sexual interactions. It can be hilarious as we dig out all the old raunchy, and some ridiculous, words that people have invented. A lot of them make dick, pussy and fuck sound boring. It serves the goal of normalizing sexuality.

I might role-play with a client in order to coach and demonstrate social skills like simple conversation and how to initiate that conversation with a woman that he's interested in. Sometimes I have clients meet me at a coffee shop with instructions to initiate a conversation as if we'd never met before, or we might go out on what would be a first dinner date with someone before coming back to the house, where generally their instruction would be to make the first move.

On one occasion I had asked the client to meet me at a small coffee shop and twenty minutes went by and he hadn't arrived. I was becoming concerned when, finally I spied him hanging around on a corner across the street, watching me through the window. Obviously, I hadn't made myself clear about coming in. Needless to say, we had to repeat the exercise at a later date.

Different exercises are required for each client depending on their presenting problem. For someone who has never had a date, just learning how to walk with a woman and take her hand, or how to put his arm around her waist, or even help her through a door can be time consuming.

A wide variety of projects and assignments might be used for a virgin with no experience, while more specific exercises would be necessary for a person with erectile difficulty or early ejaculation: like exercises to identify and surrender to arousal for ED (even Viagra doesn't always help if the client is anxious or has low libido).

We might use a scale of one-to-ten for ejaculatory control, helping the client to find and master level 6 or 7 of intensity to ride the wave of pleasure without coming.

With a client that is at a stage for enhancement, I might use a technique that I call responsive movement. It calls for both partners to use the other's touch to enhance their own pleasure, much like a cat that curves its back into the hand that pet's it. Done one at a time or together, it can become a very sensual, erotic and extremely heated dance of passion.

Also, speaking of dancing, I have taught many clients that have never dated the rudiments of dancing. I believe that it can be an important social skill. Lots of women love to dance and as I told one client, "When you're holding someone you really love and want on the dance floor, you'll thank me."

Issues that clients present can be similar, but each client deals with them differently, so I customize exercises for each person, but all structured games or practices that occur during the work are designed not only as a self-learning and growing process, but as a way for the client and myself to establish trust with one another and to become closer, and more intimate.

CHAPTER 11

JAMES

For the surrogate, a sense of nurturing is always present in this work. There is generally a lot of healing needed when a client seeks this kind of help and when the work becomes intense as it sometimes does, the nurturing place we cultivate is always there to return to, bringing reassurance with caressing, hugging, holding and talking.

Having had the experience of general caresses and getting to know one another better over a number of sessions, James and I arrived at the session where, to me, the work begins to become a little more erotic in nature.

When, if the client thinks he's ready, and I agree, we move on from the non-focused genital touching of the previous sessions, to a more focused, "show me how you touch yourself, what you like, what feels good to you?" kind of caressing. It seemed to me that James was at this point in our sessions.

But first, we needed to catch up on what he had been doing and experiencing since our last meeting.

James looked a little stressed as he settled into the pillows in the corner of my green-brown corduroy sofa. He leaned forward and took a long drink of water from his glass on the coffee table in front of us. "Man, it's been a hard week!"

"You mean emotionally or work or what?" I asked, settling beside him.

"Mostly work I guess, but I haven't been sleeping very well either and we're so busy. We're working on some new programs and there's a lot of pressure to get them finished and being tired doesn't help." He rubbed his forehead and let his hand drop limply into his lap.

"I'm sorry James. I know that you're a computer engineer of some sort, but I don't know much about that world, so I don't know what you might be going through, and I really don't know enough to even ask questions."

Shrugging, he replied, "Oh, that's okay. I'm really tired of thinking about it, anyway."

"Well, it must be worse when you can't sleep. What's going on at night? Are you just worried about work, or is there something else that's bothering you? Can you tell me?"

"I don't know, a bunch of things, I guess. It is work, but besides that I know I'm not supposed to think about it or worry, I mean, but I keep thinking that maybe this won't work. What am I gonna do then? I mean it seems natural that I should have had hard-ons sometimes in our sessions and I haven't very much. What if that keeps happening?"

He paused looking off into space, face downcast. I remained still, waiting to see what more would come.

"And on top of that, there's a new woman at work. She's nice looking and I think she's single. We've talked a couple of times and she keeps smiling at me. I don't know if she's just being friendly or if she might be interested in me... and what if she is? What do I do then? Do I just pass up another opportunity because I know nothing will work right?" He ran a frustrated hand through his hair.

"Wow, sounds like a lot going on in there." I patted his forearm lightly. "I'm sorry for the way you're feeling, but I have to tell you again that I'm not worried about it. About your ability to have erections, I mean. You just need to know how to relax your mind and feel."

James rubbed his face and eyes in exasperation. "Yeah, I know."

"Look, yes, I've said it before, but it's true and I've seen it happen time and time again and in this case, I really doubt that you'll be the exception, the only one it *doesn't* work for. In the case of this woman, if she is interested, and you want to pursue it, it's okay to take time to get to know one another before you hop into bed anyway. As a matter of fact, I would even suggest waiting a little while before you take any action at all. Just get to know her at work first. Then you'll be able to tell if you're really interested or not. Besides, that will give us some time to get a little further along."

He seemed a little relieved at my suggestion to wait. "Yeah, that's a good idea. I guess just because she might be interested in me doesn't mean I have to do something about it right now."

"Right. So, just have coffee or something at work and see how you feel. Take the pressure off. Maybe by the time you decide to ask her out, if you do, you'll feel a little more relaxed and confident about yourself. Does that feel good to you?"

"Yeah, it does, it feels better. I don't know why I got myself so wired up about it. I guess I've been feeling a little desperate." He gave a sigh, maybe of relief, or maybe he'd been breathing too shallowly, which happens when one is anxious.

"Anyway, as you say, I'll try not to worry about it right now. I'll just let myself take some time. So what's next?"

"Well, I think you need to take a minute to just breathe sweetie." I smiled. "Maybe you could practice some belly breathing, right now, huh?"

"Oh, yeah, okay. I guess that'd probably help." He settled back, relaxing deeper into the couch's pillow and closed his eyes and began taking full breaths. I watched his belly rise and fall, the silence interspersed with the sound of his soft exhale. After a bit, he opened his eyes, which had the slightly dreamy look that good breathing can bring about, and looked at me.

"Better? I asked, feeling a little relaxed and dreamy myself, just observing him.

"Better! Thanks for reminding me. It really does help."

"You're welcome. So, what else? Anything else bothering you?"

"No, not right at this moment. I feel pretty good. I'm ready."

"Great! Well, if there's nothing else you need to talk about., let's talk about us. I'd like to know how you feel about your kissing skills and if that's something you'd like to work on. Some people have boundaries around kissing, but I think in what we're doing here, it's an important part of the process. I always feel that good kisses are the first introduction to good sex."

I have had a few clients that did not want to kiss, feeling it something special that they wanted to save for their outer world relationships. However, especially for people with little or no experience, I do feel it's an important skill and as a considerably experienced and skilled kisser, I'm a good teacher.

Also, kissing is a reliable way to create passion and arousal. When I work with an occasional client that is reluctant and refuses and we are reaching for more intimacy or eroticism, it feels much drier to me. In James case, I thought it important, but I had to know how he felt about it.

"So, is that something you'd like to work on, or what do you think?" I asked.

"Well, no one's ever said anything about my kissing, but I guess I'd like to know if I'm any good or not. I've ended up in bed a couple of times, so I can't be too bad." He smiled but his eyes bespoke a lack of confidence. "But, yeah, I'd be okay with kissing."

"Good, because it falls into the area of initiating closeness and seduction. I guess I also need to know how you feel about how you do with *that*. We've been working a little each time on how you get closer, but now we need to begin expanding on it. You know, accelerating the intimacy with a woman for the first time. What do you think your comfort level would be?"

"Well, to tell you the truth, I don't know. I didn't really have to do too much those times before. The couple of women I was with sort of came on to me, so I didn't have to start anything that way. I don't know how I'd do."

He rubbed his face in his hands again and opened them to say, "God, I feel like a sixteen year old. I should have been past all this by now. Christ, I'm 40 years old!"

"Hey, you know what? Everyone feels vulnerable and nervous the first time they try to get close to someone and the important thing is you're here now, you're doing very well and by the time you leave you'll have more confidence. I know you have regrets about the past, things that do need to be acknowledged, but you can't change any of that, so don't let it take you away from the good stuff you're doing here."

I put a reassuring hand on his arm. "And you're not dead yet! You have a whole new adventure ahead and how exciting is that? It's just a change of mindset."

"Yeah, I know, it's just sometimes," his voice wandered off along with his eyes, drifting across the room.

"Well, let's practice a little more with getting close," bringing his focus back to the moment. "So let's start with what feels the most comfortable or the least scary to you. Maybe begin with what you've done in the past, like holding my hand, and we'll take it from there. All right?"

"Okay, I think I can do that much," he responded. After a moment of thought he simply moved over and put his arm around me. I rested my head on his shoulder and we sat in stillness for a minute or so. I could sense the warmth and energy between us growing until I felt him leaning his head over and turning his face down toward mine. He hovered there and I turned my face up to him, "Are you wanting to kiss me James?"

"Is it okay?"

"More than okay," I murmured.

He leaned in further. "Yeah?" and he bent down to match his lips to mine. It was a careful kiss, with just a little too much tension, and when he left, it felt slightly abrupt. Then we returned to stillness for a bit.

"Well, how was it, how'd I do?" he asked eventually, with a little bravado.

"Well, first, the lead in was great. It seemed to me that you were feeling kind of sexy for a minute there, is that true?"

He shrugged and nodded his agreement.

"Your lips are nice and soft, and you just need to relax a little more. You don't have to press quite so much. Just bring your lips to mine and do a kind of soft mushing, like when you eat a ripe strawberry and you want to keep the juice from dripping. Like this." I lifted his inner forearm to my lips and demonstrated. I kept my lips soft and loose and slightly open and lightly sucked his skin between them.

I continued, "And when you leave the kiss, you back off as though your lips want to linger, like pulling away from soft taffy. Sexy kisses aren't meant to be tidy, you know. They're sweet and delicious and from there they can become hotter, more intense and stronger. Most of the women that I know don't like tongues down their throat with the first kisses. I suppose there are probably some that do, but this is the way I like it and I think it's a good way to start. As you become more experienced, you'll be able tell what she wants. Widely parted lips are definitely a telling invitation. Anyway, shall we try it again?"

James leaned in and gave it his best try and as the kisses went on they became a little less stiff, but learning to "mush" takes a little time. Once he started feeling sexier his kisses would become sexier as well. It's all in the feeling and intention.

When we came up for air James said, "Well, I think that felt better. What do you think?"

"Definitely. And it'll get better and better with practice. The reason I showed you on your arm is because I want you to practice on your own forearm to see what it feels like and we'll do some more kissing again next week."

James tried the kisses out on his own forearm. "Hmm, well not quite the same, but I'll work on it. Your lips were so soft, I don't know if I can do that."

"Oh, I think you can, just think mushy. Besides, your own kiss felt soft as well. Now, you just have to add the intention of melting and seduction into your lips. You definitely have the potential to be a really good kisser and you know, these are just the seductive, beginning kisses. The more they go on, the hotter it will probably get and then comes tongues and really deep kissing. And that sort of comes naturally as part of your desire, I think. Anyway, more on that later, for sure."

I rose from the couch and held out my hand. "Why don't we go upstairs and pick up where we left off. Are you ready for that?"

"Yeah, let's do it."

My senses were picking up an underlying sexual energy in James that seemed waiting to come forward once he got past his fear. A good portion of my work is intuitive and I felt an occasional *something* in his vocal tone and body movements that made me think that a naturally relaxed, easily sexy man lay naked beneath the surface. We walked up the stairs holding hands.

I'd lit some incense earlier before his arrival, and the faint, spicy scent lingered in the air of the guest room. I put a CD into the stereo and the familiar sounds of "Enigma" floated out around us. James waited for me to begin undressing before he started, but within a minute we were cozily wrapped together under the soft white blanket that provided more than warmth. It also gave a sense of security and togetherness.

"This feels nice" James said, giving me a squeeze, prompting me to squeeze back. "You know, I did practice what you told me to do, trying to find the parts of my body that are most sensitive. You want me to tell you now?"

"No, I'd like to check it out and you can tell me as I go along. Where it feels erotic or especially good, and how that part likes to be touched or handled. I'll start by just touching you, okay? Like last week. Then I'll begin doing more."

After I spent a few minutes in a general non-erotic exploration of his whole body, I began the erotic focus with his head and neck, running my fingers through his hair, caressing his face and lips and feeling his ears with my fingertips. I then lowered my head to caress his face and neck with my own cheek and chin. "How's this?"

"It tickles a little. Your hair."

"Okay, then how about this?" I took his ear lobe between my lips, and applied some real kisses on his neck, "Still tickle?"

"No, it feels good," his voice was soft.

"Scale of one to ten?"

"Four."

I continued working down his body, stopping here and there to check on his responses. One place I knew he might not have checked out was his nipples. Men new to sex often bypass that area, focusing on the chest as a whole, leaving the idea of nipple stimulation to the female gender. My theory is that a nipple is a nipple, same erectile tissue, same susceptibility to stimulation, so I spent a bit of time there, touching, pinching a little, bringing it to erection.

"How about your nipples? Do you feel any sensation here?"

"Actually, yeah. I wouldn't have thought so, but yeah, a lot."

"So what feels the best? Maybe this?" I softly flipped the small erect tip, "or maybe, this?" circling it with my finger tips, "or perhaps this," giving it a light pinch (as we became more erotic I might lick or suck softly on them as well).

"I don't know, maybe you should keep on doing them all for a while," he said, suppressing a laugh.

"So I take it that's all a 5 or more?"

"Yeah, I'm surprised, but I'd say it's a five, once I get out of my head about it."

"Good." I considered my next move. "Hmmm, let me see, now." I moved down, touching his belly and sides, getting fairly low numbers on the erotic scale, to his abdomen, where I received a shiver in response. "Tickle?"

"A little"

I applied a little more pressure with my hand, "Better?"

"Yeah, but it's probably only a three."

"No such thing as *only* a three. It's all sensation and that's what we're looking for. I moved my hand down his hip to his legs, skirting his genitals for the time. Moving his legs apart a little, I traced the inside of his thighs. "And here?" I could feel the tension in his thighs.

"Uh, six?"

"Um-hmm, and what about this?" I traced my fingers up onto his balls and took them in the palm of my hand. A little shudder ran through his body. "How do you like them to be touched? Firmly like this, or lightly, or maybe just fingertips?"

"Firmly, I think, and if you kind of roll them a little in your hand? Yeah, that's good. I'd say about and 7 and a half." He made a soft little intake of breath between his teeth and a long exhale through pursed lips.

I moved up to his penis, which was taking on a bit of a life of it's own and it twitched a little in response to my touch. "Hmm, seems like this is pretty good. Can you give me a number?"

"Maybe an eight?" His face looked tight with tension.

"Relax, sweetie. Nothing's going to happen here that you don't control. Just take a deep breath." I kept my hand lightly wrapped around his penis without moving.

He took a few deep breaths until I could see the tension in his belly and legs receding.

"Do you want to stop James, or are you okay?" I asked, still not removing my hand.

He raised his head to look at me directly. "No, I don't want to stop. I like it...it's, it's just that it's really new for me, being touched like this, so I'm kind of nervous," he answered with a tight little smile.

"I know it's new James, and I don't want to push you or go too fast, so you must let me know if and when you're too uncomfortable. If we go on with this today, we'll be touching each other in ways that might be sexually arousing and it's perfectly okay if that's not all right with you. We can do something else and come back to this later. So, what do you think?"

"No, it's okay. This is what I came here to do and I want to do it," he said with some determination.

I thought to myself how sad it is that the possibility for pleasure can be so anxiety provoking to a person. "Okay, we'll go on then, but stay in touch with your feelings, okay?"

"I'll do my best." He settled back on the bed again.

His penis had relaxed in my hand, so taking an active hold again I asked, "So tell me how your dick likes to be touched. What's best?"

"Well, it all feels good, but it's especially sensitive around the head, just underneath."

I ran my fingers around the edge of the head as he suggested, and then took the shaft in my hand. "A firm touch or light touch?"

"I dunno, it all feels good, it's probably a seven or eight at this point. Do I have an erection?"

It seems that sometimes men are aware that they have one, but can't be sure of how strong it is.

His cock had obligingly responded to my explorations. "Yes, you do, but it's not too important right now, because we're just checking out what feels best and we're not really going to do much with it. So, would you feel okay about showing me how you handle yourself? That way I'll know how to handle you later."

"I guess. It feels a little weird, but okay." He reached down and took his penis, which had instantly begun to flag a little, in his hand and showed me his usual technique of stroking with a kind of spiraling motion, the same that I have observed in many men.

I did have one client that masturbated by only lightly scratching his balls and rubbing the head of his penis. The limiting of his self-pleasuring to those two areas was unusual and not conducive to allowing for sensation in actual intercourse.

When he moved his hand away, I took James' penis in my hand and imitated his movements, taking it slowly. After a minute or so the flagging penis became a flying one and I moved on to caress his body again. We were not after orgasm here.

I asked James to turn over and played with the back of his neck and his torso with my lips and ran my hands over his buttocks, checking with him for levels of sensation. Back play to me is just as important as the front of the body in sexual play and can be very sexy all on its own.

I finished up spending a little more time at the nape of his neck. It seemed to be as sensitive as my own, and it felt to me that he simply surrendered to the pleasure of it.

After awhile, I withdrew and lay down beside James and waited for him to turn over, but he simply turned his head and looked at me, his brown eyes looking dreamy again, "Nice," was all he said.

I felt myself grinning at him. "Lots of places for pleasure, don't you think?

James just grinned back and we lay together and were quiet again for a bit. But time was not on our side and if we were going to move on to showing him what I like, we would need to reverse roles. "Now I'd like to show you what feels good to me."

James dragged himself up from his dreamlike state to rest on one elbow as I rolled onto my back.

"Where would you like to start?" I asked.

"Where do you want me to start?" he parried.

I smiled up at him. "Well just start by touching, and see where that takes you. Don't forget to do what would also be enjoyable for you."

He started with his hand in my hair, stroking it softly and then began reacquainting himself with my body by running his hands slowly over me and finally came back to spend a few moments circling the shells of my ears with his fingers.

When I'm with a client it often takes a good state of relaxation for me to really feel the sensitivity of areas of my body that are not necessarily considered sexual. Breasts and genitals are usually sensitive, but all the space in between needs focused attention to sense erotic feeling. This is somewhat because, at this point in the work, I'm still part in teacher and I need to get to being more the receiver.

So I took a breath and relaxed the tension in my thighs and brought my attention to the areas under his hand or fingertips, to the warm or prickly feeling of his touch against the peach fuzz of my skin and soon I found my body responding to his touch.

When he began kissing my neck, his closeness and the feel of his breath on my skin caused anticipatory goose bumps. His lips were soft, but dry and too quick in their approach, so when he asked me if I liked that, I replied "Yes, and I'd like to tell you how it would feel even better. If you could kiss my neck like that fresh strawberry we talked about, that's what I really like. Delicious body kisses."

"Okay, let me try," and his lips on my neck began to feel softer, more open. Definitely better! Not quite there yet, but showing lots of promise.

"Well, that just jumped from a two to a four," I praised. So let's go on."

He was now sort of crouching over me and used both hands to move down my body to my breasts. Unsure of what to do, he simply ran his hands over them, and when I asked him if he would like me to show him some things I liked, he was enthusiastic in his response. I told him that my breasts are not overly sensitive as some women's are and showed him what felt the best in touches and in kisses.

I know that many women's breasts are very sensitive and some can even come to orgasm with nothing but breast stimulation, but I'm not one of them. However, there are particular ways that I enjoy breast-play, that are very enticing to my groin. I showed him and told him that on a scale of one to ten, that technique rated a six, and then I let myself just enjoy it until he was ready to move on. I tried to remain still, but my hips, my naughty betrayers, were desperate to squirm.

He moved down to my belly, touching my belly button and planting his best strawberry kisses here and there. "How's this?"

"Nice, about a seven, but before you go any further, James, let's do the backside, because when we get to my pussy, it will get a little clinical. Is that okay with you?"

"Sure. Go ahead and turn over," he agreed.

I love time spent having my whole backside caressed and by now James was developing a very nice touch so it was a pleasure to roll over to give him access to the back of my body.

On the backside I showed him how to do the biting, sucking thing on the back of my neck, that drives me absolutely wild. It's more than the sensation, which gives me chills and thrills the body; it's a kind of animal feeling of desire and helplessness wrapped in one. I've done it with many lovers and clients too, when we're further along in the relationship aspect and I've never yet had anyone not love it.

He played with the curve of my back and laid kisses on the small of it and cupped and circled my butt. I had to still my hips from rising against his hand too much and putting my butt in the air like a cat. Finally, he kind of laid on me, his face against my upper back. He felt warm and I could feel his breathing and we simply lay that way for a few minutes. It felt connected.

When he moved off of me he said, "I like your back. I like doing things to it. It's simple. Maybe safer, so it's fun. You sure like the neck thing, huh? That was fun, once I felt like I could do it right."

"Yeah, I do like it. You liked it too, when I did it to you, I could tell. So, let's get back to the front." I turned over and asked James to come and sit between my legs. As he situated himself I reached for a pillow and asked him to help me get it under my hips.

"Are you okay there, James? Are you comfortable?" He nodded. "First, I'd like to tell you that I've done this a lot of times, but it always feels a little vulnerable for me. Just so that you know if you're feeling a little unsure, that I'm having some feelings of my own, too."

"Really? Well would you rather not do this?"

"No, no, it's fine," I assured him. "I just wanted you to know, and now that I've done that, I'm fine to go ahead. So I'd like you to begin by just touching me or stroking me." He obliged by putting his hand on one of my bent knees.

I went on. "I'm going to acquaint you with my pussy and show you how mine works. Every woman is different in what they like and what works for them, so don't assume you should know any thing more than some basic things. We'll talk as we go along about how you could ask a woman what she likes, and how to do it, but for now, I'll tell you about my body."

I had him stroke and massage in ways that I like and showed him how the labia begin to swell as arousal rises. After a bit, I showed him where my hidden clitoris is which can sometimes be daunting to a nervous client, and how to stimulate it. Then I invited him to just play awhile, touching and caressing in ways that were also interesting and fun for him. To allow himself to enjoy doing what he was doing and not doing it just for me.

I told him I'd let him know when something felt especially good, or also if something was uncomfortable and I had him use some lubricant to facilitate what he was doing.

He had a soft, non-invasive, friendly kind of touch. It didn't have any of the sharpness to it that I have found with some people's energy. Poky fingers are the worst, to me; fingers that are too sharp, too direct, too rough on tender flesh. I prefer some subtlety, especially at first. Later though, when things are getting hot, a little rougher can be exciting and fun.

"You have a very nice touch, James. That all feels good. In fact, it feels really, really good." He had paid attention to the lesson in clitoral stimulation.

"I don't need the stimulation to go any further right now though. I'd like to move on. So, I'd like you to put more lube on your fingers and when you're ready, put one finger inside me."

James used the lube as I suggested and then with a look of extreme concentration, looked for and found the vaginal opening and slowly inserted a finger.

"Good, go slow. Do you feel the band or ring of muscles right at the opening? Aside from the G spot, that is where I get the most vaginal stimulation, right there at the opening. I have had a hysterectomy and I don't have a cervix for any stimulation, so inside it's pleasurable and I feel pressure that feels good, but the main point of stimulation along with that is either the G spot or the opening. G spot stimulation with a penis of course, requires some manipulation of position."

I instructed James to push his finger further and to just explore all around to see what he could feel.

At different points I would tell him what felt the best, which pressure felt more subtle, which more direct.

Then I guided him to the G spot, just inside and above the pubic bone, and showed him different strokes that I really liked: The scoop, the short stroke and the roundabout. The scoop up and back toward the one stimulating is slow and sensual, the short stroke, rubbing the spot fairly vigorously with small movements either forward and back or side to side, is more direct and the roundabout circles the whole vagina and sweeps across the G spot.

James' actions were feeling very good, but we were running out of time, nor was it the right moment to go any further. It had been a very full session and I thought James would probably be pretty saturated. From the look on his face he seemed to be enjoying himself, partly watching me, partly just experiencing.

"Okay m'dear. I think we need to finish now. Are you ready to remove yourself from my body, sir?"

He grinned and pulled his fingers away. "Well, that was interesting. And you know what? I realize that I never got to spend any time doing this stuff. It seems like it was mostly get a hard on and screw, which you know, didn't really work for me. I liked that you seemed to like it."

"Yeah, I did, and you were learning fast. Now, I'm sorry to say that our time is just about up, but let's take time for a quickie cuddle."

James lay down and opened his arms to fold them around me. I turned to face him and slung a leg over his, noticing in the process a slight erection, a "chubby" pressing against me. "How are you feeling?"

"Good, but it made me realize how much I don't know. Makes me wish I had done more, those times I was with those other women. Maybe they would have liked it more, or maybe if I had taken more time I would've kept my hard on."

"That's probably true. Hurrying toward the goal doesn't leave much time or room for good strong arousal. At least until you learn to trust your dick. Then you'll probably be able to have some of those hot quickies. But, I can tell you that when you leave this work, you'll know a lot and I think you'll be a good lover. You just need some knowledge and experience and confidence. Not to worry, okay? Any questions I can answer quickly?"

"No, not right now. Maybe next time after I've had time to think about all of this. It feels like a lot."

"Yeah, we took a big jump this session. So, continue with your homework that I gave you before, practice your arm kissing and next time, I'll give you something else as well. Now, it's time to get our selves up and get you on your way. I had a good time today and it seemed like you did too, huh?"

"Yeah, I did." He smiled, eyebrows up and nodded vigorously. We both rose and dressed and James went on downstairs to write his check, while I took the sheet off the bed and redressed it with the green and gold comforter and pillows.

Giving the room a last glance for neatness and pre-client condition, I made my way downstairs to find James waiting for me at the door where he hugged me warmly and gave me a small goodbye kiss, before turning his attention to the outside world. "Thanks so much for helping me. I'm starting to feel like it might work."

"Oh sweetie, you're so welcome. I'm really happy for you that you're doing this. And you're doing good work. It's a pleasure to spend time with you."

"Thanks, Cheryl. See you next week?"

"Yep, I'll be here. Have a good week James! Try not to stress and hey, maybe have a cup of coffee with that woman at work!"

He shrugged saying "I'll have to see how I feel. Maybe I will."

I took my sign down as he exited and smiled as he turned to give me a goodbye wave. We were getting closer, becoming more intimate, beginning to feel like friends. Just what needed to happen at this point.

CHAPTER 12
JAMES

"So, how're you doing James. How's your week been? Had any fun? I stepped back from our hug and we made our way from the entryway into the living room and headed for the couch.

"Well, we're still really busy, but things are going along alright. I saw a couple of movies on the weekend and just kind of relaxed."

My big, fluffy, orange cat Sammy presented himself to James for adoration, walking back and forth under James' hand, waving and displaying his bushy tail like a banner.

"How you doin' big guy? Chillin?" James asked him as he rubbed Sammy's head with both hands. Sammy responded with head rolls and would have stayed like that forever, so we finally both pushed him away and he walked away with feathery tail waving high with dignity. Such a pleasure slut! He had a lot to teach us.

We settled in on the couch and talked about movies we'd seen for a few minutes and just chatted about life in general for both of us. I asked if he had been talking to the woman at work that had seemed interested in him and he said that he had, that they'd been talking a bit and that she had made reference to a boyfriend.

"Oh well", I said, "it's all practice."

"Yeah, it's okay. I'm actually kind of relieved, and you know, maybe a little disappointed too, but I know I'm not ready yet anyway. I've got a ways to go. I'd like to feel more confident before I really start trying to meet women, but I'll keep trying to talk and be social."

I had just started wondering if James would act on his assignment from last time to be the one to make first contact, when he turned more toward me and put his arm on the back of the couch and softly touched my neck as we talked.

That continued for a few minutes and finally James asked, "How can I get closer? Should I just move over?"

I suggested he try it and see if it felt relatively comfortable. He did and it seemed it felt okay because we ended up in a hug and eventually in some kissing. He still needed more relaxation in his kisses, but progress had definitely been made. He must have been doing his homework.

I told him that it was okay to stroke my body, in preparation for becoming more passionate, making out and getting clothes off. In the beginning it feels more like practice or an exercise, but after awhile, once a client becomes more confident and allows himself to feel, rather than do, the passion usually takes over.

Also, genuine arousal occurs more easily once his confidence allows him to see me less as teacher and more as erotic partner. Something that almost always happens.

After we kissed and touched on the couch for a while I said, "Well, this is really nice, but how are you going to get me to the bedroom?"

He looked taken aback for a moment. "I don't know. I could say 'Let's go to the bedroom?'"

Laughing I said, "Yeah, that's the direct approach and it's good but, you could also say something like 'Let's go get more comfortable on the bed or why don't we take this to the bedroom.' I'm sure there are some great lines and maybe you could ask Dr. Johnston about it. I know he probably has some good ones. He's certainly been around in his time. Actually, this is only needed if she's letting you take the lead. Who knows, you could be with a woman who jumps on you and takes *you* to the bedroom. Now wouldn't that be fun?"

"Yeah, I think! Maybe not yet, but it's something to look forward to. But for now, let's go to the bedroom," he laughed. James was really cute when he was re-laxed. He took my hand and pulled me off the couch and we headed for the stairs.

When we reached the bedroom, I turned around to James and said, "Let's start here," as I put my arms around him, pressed my body to his and lifted my face for a kiss. It's good to surprise them once in awhile. He bent a bit to kiss me and we stood wrapped togeth-er, the kisses getting better and better.

Finally, when I said, "Let's go to the bed," James walked me backwards and we fell in a heap on it, laughing. We helped each other out of our clothes and threw ourselves up onto the pillows, where James put his arms around me and cuddled up next to me. It felt like we had moved to a new level of mutual comfort and confidence.

I knew that James felt more comfortable giving than receiving, so now that we had covered some of the basics of mine and his, the next step, in my opin-ion, needed to be his learning to let go and surrender to sensation and intimacy while on the receiving end of things.

We turned to lay face-to-face, my leg over his, hold-ing each other and stroking one another's bodies. We kissed some more and the more relaxed he became, the more arousing the kisses were becoming.

Finally, I said, "You know what I'd like to do? I'd like to just be in charge for while of giving you pleasure. Do you think you can stand that? Just lay back and enjoy and receive? Later we can turn it around, but for now, it's just about you and what you feel and I get the pleasure of taking charge of your body."

"Okay, yeah. I think I'd like that," he said.

"Would oral sex be okay as part of this?" I always ask, because contrary to belief, everyone is not comfortable with this part of lovemaking.

"A blow job? Hell, yeah!"

Not my favorite term I thought, but hey, that's me. "Let's think of some other terms we can use as well. How about getting or giving head, or going down on you or even sucking your cock? You know, just so that you have a repertoire. Different terms for different times, you know? I think for me at least, hearing my lover say 'I want you to suck my cock, or give me head' makes me feel sexier than 'Give me a blow job.' Unless, of course I'm feeling a little tough or raunchy that day." I grinned at James and he grinned back.

"Yeah, when I'm feeling that way 'How 'bout a blow job, baby' could be a turn on. It all depends on what's going on at the moment, but I think it's better to err on the side of caution, until you know. At least in the beginning, know what I mean? Anyway, your lover of the moment is me and now I've told you what I like best."

James took it in his stride. "Sure, I understand. I guess maybe it sounds like a kind of a guy term, huh? Anyway, I haven't had too much experience with it, but I'd like to try it."

"Great." I rose up to bring my knee between his legs, so that my body hovered over his, my breasts lightly brushing his chest. "So, it's my turn to be in charge now, right? All you have to do is relax and enjoy, but sounds and movement will be appreciated and rewarded with great fervor on my part." I leaned over to kiss him.

His mouth was open, soft and pliant, so different than when he felt he had to do something and the kiss felt as though we drank from one another. A beautiful start! I moved across and down his body, kissing and licking and also at the same time, noticing a certain amount of tension in his arms and belly.

"Keep breathing James. Let your body go." The tone of my voice sounded sultry to me as my sensual self stepped forward. As he followed my suggestion, I could feel his tension easing. "Try moving your body a little, if you feel tight. Maybe if you can move in response to what I'm doing, it might relax you."

I continued to move down his body and when I got to his cock, teased around his thighs and balls, until his arousal was obvious enough to slip a condom on him. I always keep them ready at the side of the bed, so reaching over and sliding it on is only a short interruption and I try to make the doing of it as sexy as possible, making eye contact and almost a little production of it. Just to keep it part of the fun, rather than being too businesslike.

Although I believe that a lot of people don't use condoms for oral sex, I use them for everything involving body fluids. I feel that on a professional level, it gives my clients a feeling of safety, knowing that I don't take any risks. Knowing that I am safe also gives them more freedom to practice oral sex with me if they wish to do it without protection. Of course, the client and I always discuss whether they have cold or canker sores prior to any oral sex.

There are many variations one can use during oral sex, using both mouth and hands, interrupting a consistent movement with the lavishing of great licks and swirls or even lightly tapping the penis against a flat tongue. It can, and in my opinion, for the giver's pleasure, should be a creative project. The best oral sex for me as the giver means eventual watery eyes and a runny nose, if my partner can last long enough.

As I began to pleasure James orally, his body began to tighten again and he lay completely still. I encouraged him to let his hips move, even if it felt strange at first, to become a partner in his own pleasure. He began doing so, a little cautiously and then after a bit, he started to get into the rhythm I was creating, which in the beginning was slow, drawn out and sensual. I would occasionally put one hand on his heart to keep an intimate connection.

I listened to the sounds he made and to his breathing for the quickening breaths that would tell me orgasm was impending, so I could speed up or slow down depending on what I heard. An orgasm would be the end and we were after long-term pleasure. Besides, holding off on it, sustaining arousal, makes for more mind-blowing orgasms at the end of lovemaking.

Finally, I could tell that he was definitely getting very close, but he himself reached out and put a hand with stop in it, on my head. "Better stop now," he croaked. Since that was in keeping with my idea I raised my head and sat up, but left a calming hand cupped on his genitals. I learned that in Tantric sex classes long ago and find it to be very comforting, especially after orgasm, but also find that it has a calming effect when orgasm is delayed.

"You know James, it's okay to come, but I'd like to keep the energy for today. I do want you to know though, that if it should ever happen all of a sudden, that's fine. No big deal, okay?"

I moved up and lay down beside James again, putting my hand on his chest. He took hold of it and pressed it to his body. "That was great! I could have come a few times, but every time, you'd do something different and the feeling would go down. I've only had it once and it wasn't like that. Matter of fact, I don't think I gave it time enough to really get into it, or maybe it just didn't last long enough."

I raised myself up on one elbow to look at him. "Did it last long enough for you then, to come?"

"No. It felt like I didn't have a good enough erection so she sort of stopped and we went back to kissing."

"Well, you didn't seem to have much problem today. See, I think it's the relaxation. So, let's calm down for a few minutes and then I need to ask you how you feel about practicing oral sex with me. Is it within your boundaries? It doesn't have to be part of the program, but it's a good thing to have some skill with it."

He frowned. "I don't know how I feel about it. I mean, it seems pretty personal and maybe something I'd only want to do with a girlfriend. I mean, do all women expect that?"

"Well, would you expect to get it from her?" I asked.

He looked at me with a slightly surprised eyebrow. "Yeah, well, it seems like women giving men head happens more. I see it in movies and people talk about it more than the other way around. But aren't there some women that don't like getting head?"

"I suppose there are some, but I think most women expect that you would want to do it. Besides it's one way in lovemaking that she gets to lie back and just be pleasured."

He sat up with his feet over the side of the bed, on the floor. I could feel his agitation. "Well, I don't know if I want to do it. Couldn't I just learn with a girlfriend?"

I sat up on the bed myself, aware that we'd stumbled on a hurdle. "Yes, you could, but frankly at your age most women expect you to have a little skill in everything to do with sex. Look I'm not trying to talk you into this. I don't have anything to gain. I just wouldn't be doing my job if I didn't introduce it, and to my way of thinking, it's just as important as anything else that I could teach you."

"Well, what about diseases and things. His voice sounded angry. "I didn't come here to catch something."

Ouch, that stung! Keeping my own reactions in check I replied calmly but emphatically, "If I wasn't sure of my safeness, I wouldn't be bringing this up. I'm a professional therapist. I can't afford to go around giving clients any kind of disease. In addition to that, I have my own relationship to protect. I have to keep myself safe."

"I'm sorry" he said, leaning over to put his chin in his hand, "That didn't come out exactly the way I meant, but I just don't know if I want to. I guess it scares me."

"Fair enough, I understand and we can continue to talk about it if you like. It isn't something that we have to do, but it does have to do with knowing how to please a woman. Maybe you need to think about it."

James sighed and nodded. "Yeah, I think so."

"That's really fine, James. But, since this has come up, there are things you need to do to take care of yourself, not only here, but in any possible sexual situation. First is the safe sex talk. Before you decide to do anything without protection, you have to know your partner's sexual history, what kind of people she's had sex with and if she's always used protection. Does she have any history of herpes, or any other contagious diseases? Has she had HIV tests with negative results? Then you both have HIV tests and maybe even tests for std's before you go in with no rain hat. If you didn't know when she had sex last, and you wanted to be really safe, you'd continue to use condoms and have another HIV test in another 6 months or so, as it doesn't always show up right away. Remember, when you have sex with her, you're having sex with everyone she's ever been with.

So that you know, I have HIV tests regularly, even though I use condoms, and have always had negative results and I have no STD's. I use condoms for everything that I do with a client, so that they know that I am safe and on top of that, if a client is more comfortable giving me oral sex using safety precautions, there are things we can use. There is a chance of HIV transmission through oral sex, but the research I've seen says it's fairly minimal."

He had turned to look at me as I talked, leaning back a little on the bed, resting on one hand. He frowned slightly. "I dunno, it doesn't seem very spontaneous to go bringing up her sex life"- he flushed– "or mine." He thought about that for a moment or two then asked, rather grumpily I thought, "Like what? What kind of things would you use for oral sex on a woman?"

I answered his observation first. "James you need to talk about your sex lives first, before you get to actual sex of any sort. You wouldn't be discussing the practical issues while you're having sex. If it's also that you're uncomfortable talking about your own lack of experience we can talk about how to best handle that later on, but the sex history conversation is an important one to have. Now, in answer to your question about what to use for protection in oral sex with a woman, there are dental dams, which are sort of like condoms but a little thicker or you can use an actual condom by cutting it open and spreading it across the labia. My personal choice is plastic wrap. You can see through it and I can feel the mouth more and I think the giver feels more too. I don't know how your partner would feel about you hauling out your box of plastic wrap though." That got a smile.

"Hmm, maybe you should tell Glad Wrap. It could be a new ad for them. They could make a new one and call it Glad pussy wrap." Jokes; a corny one but, nevertheless, a joke. This was good. His anger was fading.

Whatever he decided, at least it felt like we were beginning to get back on good ground together.

"The really important thing James, is that it's incredibly important to know about your partner. I don't allow oral sex on me if my client has a cold sore or even a canker sore. Better to put it off."

"Well, I'm here to learn about sex and I guess that's a part of it, right? But, you know, I would like to think about it. If I do, it will probably be with the plastic wrap. Would that be okay with you?"

"Sure, that's fine."

"I guess I'm afraid I'm not going to like it and then what, if women expect it?"

"Well, we'll cross that bridge when you've made a decision." I'm curious though, "What is it that you're afraid you won't like?"

"Oh, I don't know. It just seems weird and I guess I'm afraid of the smell or taste. It's just sort of bizarre. It's all sort of closed in."

"Yeah, and I'm sure it must seem like a big mystery. We are built differently than you with everything hidden away. But, until you decide to give it a try, its all just speculation, so why don't you give it some thought and we can talk about it later."

James was quiet for a few moments, looking down at his feet on the floor. His brown hair lay tousled on the top of his head and his forehead was crumpled into little wrinkles between his eyes. "I feel like I'm supposed to want to do this and I feel like there's something wrong with me, if I don't."

"I don't think any of that is true. It's just a matter of preferences. I'm not pushing you to like it, sweetie. You may finally decide that you aren't into it, but the truth is that you won't know until you experiment with it and as an experiment, this is the best place to do it." I paused a moment.

"You know there's another element to this too. When you see that you're giving pleasure to your partner, it makes it all more fun and definitely worth the doing."

He kept his eyes on the floor and I could feel the resistance oozing off of him.

Keeping my voice calmer than felt I said, "Look, I'm not trying to force you into this and it's not like I'm seeking oral sex for myself. I don't need to. But it is a usual part of lovemaking and I think you owe it to yourself to at least familiarize yourself with it and try it out. If you do and you really can't get into it, then fine, that's your preference, but at this point you don't know. It's sort of like going all the way to another country and never trying the food. It's an adventure, and you've come all this way to learn. Is it possible you could think of it like that?"

"I don't know, maybe."

He smoothed his hair down and turned again to look at me, his brown eyes concerned and reached out, laying his hand on mine. "I hope this doesn't make you feel bad. It's not about you, really, it's me. I know you're trying to help me. It's just, I guess I'm feeling nervous, and stupid!"

The tension in my belly rushed out like a long held breath and I felt the soft brush of compassion again. "I'm sorry. I know you're feeling awkward, but I'm not feeling bad. It's okay, it's just something you don't know about and you don't have to make a decision now. As a matter of fact, it feels more comfortable to me for both of us, if you give it some time."

I took his hand. "For now I'd just like to go back to just getting close again. Can we do that? Could we cuddle for a bit?" I stretched out on the bed, feeling relief, in both body and emotions and held out my arms to be filled with his body.

"Yeah, that sounds good." His voice held relief as well. He moved down to lie facing me and pulled me close to him. His body felt chilly on mine, so I felt around for our blanket and pulled it over us. Both of us kicked at it with our feet to get them covered and finally we lay cozy and safe, our arms wrapped around each other. We'd made it through a difficult place and come out the other side together.

"I am going to think about it," whispered in my ear.

"I'm sure you will," I murmured back, and we lay quietly, simply breathing one another in, for the remainder of our time.

CHAPTER 13

JAMES

James sat down on the couch and placed the little brown bag he'd brought on the coffee table and after giving Sammy his obligatory scratch and rub, picked it up again. "This is for you."

"Ooh, yea, for me?" As I opened the bag, a faint, but distinct aroma wafted out.

"Umm, I smell something good. Chocolate?"

"Yeah, I just thought you might like it."

"I love chocolate. Who doesn't? I pulled out a small packet, wrapped in transparent paper, of what looked like chocolate covered wafers. The label read 'Chocolate caramel graham cookies.'

"Thank you so much! This is so sweet! Shall we have one?"

"Sure, I haven't tried them either." he said.

I opened the package and he took one from me. I took one for myself and we nibbled the delicious little treat as we also began to talk.

"So, I've been thinking," James said, settling back on the sofa, "about what we talked about last time."

"You mean about the oral sex question?" He nodded, chewing on his cookie.

"Wow, this is good!" I licked my fingers clean of chocolate "How about we see what's going on with us first, before we talk about that, okay? How has your week been?"

"Well, I know I said I didn't feel ready yet, but I started looking at some dating services and ended up joining one. I kind of surprised myself, but I thought I'd just check it out," he said, almost matter of factly, as he did his own chocolate clean up of his fingers.

"Oh, really? I thought you were just going to relax about dating for awhile."

"Well, I thought so too, but I just wanted to see what it was like and I actually ended up emailing a couple of women and even talked to one of them on the phone and now I've got a coffee date this weekend. Just to meet."

I sat back, a little amazed. "Wow, great! Unexpected, but good for you!" I patted his knee. "You're full of surprises! Well, how are you feeling about it? Are you nervous? Or how do you feel?"

"Well, yeah, I'm pretty nervous. But you know what? I realize that the reason I could do it at all, is that I'm feeling like I'm going to be okay eventually and I keep telling myself that I don't have to commit to anything. I'm just trying to treat it as seeing if we might want to have a real date, you know, if we're attracted to each other. From her picture, she's pretty and I enjoyed talking to her, but I don't know, who knows if she'll like me in person, or if I'll like her. But at least I'm starting to put my feet in the water and that feels good."

"Hey, it's a big step and you're moving along pretty well, so this is a good time to at least be looking into it. After all, even if you do find someone you like, you don't have to jump in to bed right away. You can take your time, until you feel ready." I reached out to squeeze his arm for reassurance.

"Yeah, thanks, I need to remember that. Otherwise it's overwhelming, right now. I'll just try to take it one meeting at a time and see what happens," he said with a shrug.

Then, as if he suddenly remembered his now ongoing assignment to make the first contact, he reached across the narrow space between us and took my hand in his. His hand felt warm, the palm slightly moist. He watched as he ran his thumb over the top of my fingers, tracing the outlines of the fingernails and I could feel a shift in his energy, a softening.

Then he lifted his eyes to meet mine and grinned, "See, I didn't forget. I'd like to talk more about the dating stuff, but not right now. Right now I have to work on my assignment, if that's okay with you? Let's see, what do I do next? Oh yeah, I move over like this."

He scooted closer to me and put his arm around me and squeezed a bit. "This feels pretty good!" His voice held that soft, teasing quality of that other James, the potential James, that popped in and out of our time together, always a surprise. This James gave me a lot of confidence about his sexual future. It doesn't happen like this with many, but as a client becomes more comfortable with himself and with me, various degrees of the sexual aspect of their nature usually begins to emerge. Of course, some are more fun than others and I was beginning to suspect that James might be one of those fun ones.

"How about some kissing? Shall we make out?" His voice still held that teasing tone. I said I'd love to and he leaned into me and after an awkward moment of positioning his head to reach my lips, began to practice his best strawberry kisses. He was getting to be a good kisser and I could feel myself responding. It's a good sign when I can quit thinking about the kisses and simply enjoy them.

We made out for a while, and I ended up lying back on the couch with James squeezed next to me, his knee between my legs. Clearly, if this was to go any further we needed to go upstairs. I made an effort to slow the energy, pulling back my response a bit and he caught the hint. "Upstairs?"

"Yeah, upstairs," I smiled, delighted that he made the call.

He stood and held out his hand to help me up and we took the stairs up to our little boudoir, where we threw ourselves on the bed and continued with our make out session. I suggested that James practice getting our clothes off while we kissed and soon, with a little and coaching here and there again, we were both skin to skin, once more.

We lay chest to breast and belly to belly. The soft curls of hair on his chest, tickled my nipples and his burgeoning, definitely interested cock, nudged fervently at my pubic bone. "This feels really nice," he sighed.

I pulled my head back to look at him. "Yes, it does, but if it's okay with you, I feel like now we need to talk about what thoughts you had during the week about the oral sex question. That way we can move on, one way or another. Are you ready to deal with that now? We could just take a little break, here."

"Sure." He shifted his body slightly, creating some space between us. We had generated some heat and I could now feel a whisper of cool air on my belly. "Well, I thought about what you said: That most women would expect oral sex and expect me to have an idea of what I was doing. I guess that's probably true and if I don't practice it here with you, at this stage, I might end up trying it for the first time, on someone I don't know, or trust, as well as you. So, I've decided that I'd like to try with you and if I don't like it, then I hope it's okay. But do you mind if I start with the plastic wrap? Then, I'll see how I feel."

"Of course, that's fine. I appreciate that you trust me James. Are you thinking about trying it today?"

The first time I introduce oral sex to a client, it always starts fairly clinically. Getting them used to the idea. Taking it slowly, showing them what to do and things that might feel good to their partner, but primarily just allowing them to discover for themselves that this could be enjoyable and maybe even fun.

"Yeah, might as well," he replied, awkwardly shrugging his shoulders. Unfortunately, it didn't appear to relieve the anxious tension I detected in his body.

"Alright, then, let me get the plastic wrap." I disengaged myself and reached under the bed and pulled it out.

Startled, James asked "Do you always keep it there?"

"Nope, just for you my dear. Just in case. I didn't want to run downstairs. And, I thought that you might decide to try it."

"Okay, so what do we do?"

I pulled a short length of wrap from the box and tore it off. "Let's put this to the side for a moment and then I'd like you to put yourself between my legs."

I floated the wrap with two fingers, like a little parachute, and laid it carefully on the opposite side of the bed, then pulled a pillow over and put it underneath my hips, and lay back with my knees up as James lifted himself to move into position.

James sat on one hip watching me, his face expressionless, and when I beckoned with one finger, he moved closer between my legs and sat with his legs folded underneath him and rested his hands on my knees. This wasn't the first time he'd been here, but I knew that this time he felt more awkward. Way too much buildup!

"Are you okay, James?" I asked. "Ready to go on?"

"Yeah, I feel okay. What shall I do?" His palms felt sweaty on my knees.

"Well, why don't you begin by leaning in a little closer and just breathe and see how you feel with my scent."

He bent forward and took a few breaths, then looked up at me. "I don't smell much, mostly just a little perfume. It's okay!" I was a bit amused by his surprise.

"Good, but you know, different women have different degrees of scent. I just don't happen to have very much and it varies at different times. But it seems you're okay so far, so to continue, before the plastic wrap, why don't you spend a bit kissing my thighs and working your way down."

His kisses were tentative, unsure, not the soft, open mouth kisses I knew him capable of, and his brow had that little furrow again as he kissed one thigh and moved to the other, stopping just before the juncture of my thigh and groin each time. I could tell he was nervous.

"Still alright," I asked.

"Yeah, I think so." He leaned on one elbow and looked up at me, a shy almost embarrassed look on his face. "I think I'm ready for the plastic wrap. Might as well give it a try now." His tone sounded resigned to getting the job done. An attitude I hoped might change.

"Okay, well it's right there, if you'll get it." I directed.

He picked it up, holding it on the corners, delicately. "Do I just lay it over you?"

"Yeah, just spread it over the important parts."

I could hear the softest of crinkling noises from the wrap as he laid it down and began to position it over me. I helped him keep it straight and showed him how to press it between the labia, for more sensation for both of us and then told him to hold the edges in place.

"When you're ready, start on the outside of my yoni and work your way in. Use your whole mouth, like you would if you were kissing, soft wet kisses and use your tongue. Just be playful, do what you feel like doing and I'll give you some guidance as well."

A good student as always, James explored. I could see his closed eyes, just above my pubic bone, his head bobbing and weaving between my legs. His mouth even through the plastic wrap felt warm and smooth and I could feel little ripples of arousal in my belly.

He lifted his head to look at me. "Can you feel this?"

"Yes, even through the plastic it feels nice. Why don't you see if you can find my clitoris," I suggested.

"Okay, but you know, I can't tell too much with the wrap, what I'm feeling through it," He set his tongue back to its exploration, making the end of it stiff and pointy and poked around in the general area.

"Is this it?" he asked, pushing hard with his tongue.

"Yes that's it, but you don't have to work so hard at it. Just lick around in circles."

He tried to relax his tongue and made some circles and even did some vertical licks, but after a couple of minutes, suddenly sat up, a frown on his face. "You know what? This feels kind of silly and the plastic is in the way."

"Well, yeah, that was the point of using the wrap, I think, but do you want to stop?" I tried to keep my voice steady, though his perturbed face did make me want to laugh.

He sat back with his hands braced on the front of his thighs, pushing his shoulders up and looked at me directly. "No, I don't think so. I think I want to try it without the plastic wrap. It doesn't feel so weird to me now."

"Really?" I asked, "Are you sure?". This does almost always happen, when starting out with the plastic. It gets discarded pretty quickly as the idea loses its strangeness. In our case, the wrap just seemed to give a needed sense of security to get started.

His response was to remove it, wad it up and put it aside. Then, lowering his body, he began kissing my thighs. It seemed as though making this decision had given him a little more enthusiasm, because his kisses had definitely become more inspiring to me.

After planting a soft kiss or two on my pubic bone, he tentatively began his own explorations and I left him alone to experience it for him self and to make his own discoveries. This first run was just to get him used to it and to see if this was something he would like. The best lovers are the ones that really enjoy what they're doing, after all!

I have to say, although there is sensation with the plastic wrap, more than with any other protection, there's nothing like the real thing and the silky feeling of a soft wet tongue.

After a few minutes he raised his head, his face flushed and his lips pink. "How was that?"

"Well, for me, it felt soft and warm and I could definitely feel the beginning of a stirring. What you were doing was really nice, but, how was it for you? Any surprises, good or bad?"

This is always a pretty vulnerable question, because no woman wants to hear any bad news about her self. Sometimes I'm amazed that I can ask it, but honesty about his feelings was important here.

"Well. even though I didn't know what I was doing, I was surprised at how easy it was. It felt strange at first. The skin down there's so soft and it feels really different. I didn't taste much, and after I got used to the idea that I was actually doing it, it was nice, actually. You smelled good and I didn't mind anything about it like I thought I might. You know, I've thought about it a lot, but never thought I'd do it. So, what kind of things should I do? That women like, that you like?"

I felt increasingly confident that when he got the hang of everything, he would be a good lover; always willing to try and learn and without the constant resistance that I encounter with some clients, the ones I feel like I'm dragging, with them kicking and screaming, into heaven.

"Well, feel free to play some more. This time you could start out with some delicious body kisses first. That would be yummy and you can work your way around to doing whatever you like and when you want to know what I like, you can ask me, in the moment."

"Just ask if you like it?" he said, looking doubtful.

"Sure, or you could also say, 'Tell me what feels good, what feels the best for you. Show me what you like.' If you want to really please her, you have to know what turns her on, what does it for her. And, in the end, she'll love you for it, when you know how to hit her hot spots."

The chameleon he was becoming smiled, one eyebrow raised.

"Okay, coach, here I come." He started to crawl up my body kissing my belly and breasts with a warm, open and moist mouth and I could feel that other man, the hidden lover making little forays onto my body. Even a small increase in James' confidence opened a door for that man, and he would emerge, a glint in his eye.

James was actually learning fast and it was beginning to be very enjoyable. "Is this what you mean, these kinds of kisses?"

"Oh yeah!" I gave a little wiggle, in response.

He continued moving around various places before finally beginning a descent and landing softly back between my legs, where he continued with his previous exploration. I lay back, enjoying the action, but waiting to see if he would be able to ask me questions. It seemed he remembered some of what I liked with fingers and tried to do the same with his mouth.

After a couple of minutes, he rested his head on my thigh to ask, "Is this okay? Should I do something else? What would you like?"

Great! He was asking. I responded by telling him how I liked to be pleasured: different speeds and things to do with his mouth.

He would try something and then ask, "How's this?" The asking was the right thing for now, but "how's this," had gotten to be a little repetitive.

Since the spoken word is very stimulating to me, and I suspect to many women, I asked him to begin making it a little more personal, a little more connected to me, his partner of the moment, by saying something like: "Is this good for you? or 'Is there a way I can make it better for you?" And adding, "baby" in there somewhere may sound hokey, but in the middle of everything, it can be really sexy. To me, at least. I use it on men myself, sometimes, as in: "Does it feel good baby?" or "What do you want baby?" It makes me feel sultry and strong and it adds to the ambiance, lets me feel in charge, and keeps me turned on. My partners either like it, or they at least don't mind. I figure anything that keeps *me* turned on is only a benefit to them anyway.

"It's always good to let your partner know that you're enjoying what you're doing too, James. Occasional sounds are good or tell her that she smells good, or tastes good or that you love her pussy. It's a big charge for the woman to know that her lover really enjoys her body. It's empowering and a big turn on to hear a guy enjoying himself, definitely more exciting than if he's doing it just to get her hot. Know what I mean?"

He nodded a definite affirmative. "Yeah, that makes sense."

"So, how do you feel about talking or making sounds?" I prompted him.

"Well, It's not something I've really thought about, so I'll have to see, but I'll work on it. Now, let's see what can I do here to make you feel good? Hmmm, guess I'll have to check it out, myself."

And, there he was again, the shadow lover, teasing me. If this guy came out to play more often, we could really have fun! Check it out he did and I just quit being the watcher and let myself enjoy and heard myself making some pleasure sounds of my own.

"So, coach, what do you think? Am I doing okay? It seems like maybe you're enjoying it. I really like feeling your body move and listening to you. You make sounds too and I see what you mean about the turn on factor. It's hot to hear it." He seemed pretty delighted or excited, I couldn't quite tell the difference.

"Yeah, I do and if my body is happy, it's moving. So, you're definitely doing really well, James. What do you think?"

"I think I am too. So far, I like everything I've tried and I'm starting to feel a lot better about myself. It feels like a door that's been closed has swung open...not all the way yet, but I feel like I'm beginning to see a different world out there. I feel really great, right now!" He smiled a happy grin and sat back looking very satisfied with himself.

"Wonderful," I encouraged and held my arms open to him. "Now come up and snuggle with me for a few minutes before you go."

"Okay," he complied and curled up against me. "There's one thing. I notice that even though I liked what I was doing and what you were doing too, with your body, I didn't have much of a hard on. Should I be worried about that?" He laid his head on the pillow, settling one arm underneath my neck and the other around my body.

"Know what? In my experience, it's not unusual. Sometimes when you're so focused on what you're doing in giving pleasure, the energy isn't in your dick. But I bet if we were up to intercourse and I were to say 'Come up here and fuck me' it would rise to the occasion. But anyway, not to worry. Worry doesn't work, as you know. Just let go of it. It's not important today."

I sighed and cuddled in closer. "Relax, sweetie and let's just be together for a few minutes, before I have to throw you out into the cold, cruel world."

He laughed a little and we lay together, just holding each other, listening to our breathing, with an occasional small kiss or nuzzle. It felt warm and caring.

A short while later, I gave James a last squeeze and we ended our session with another friendly kiss and rose, accompanied by the beeping of my little alarm clock by the bed, telling us it was time to do just that.

I dressed quickly and had pulled the sheet off, replacing it with the bedspread, when he came back from the bathroom, to dress. Sammy, the cat, wandered in to see what was going on, since he had been shut out from the bedroom, and demanded his final ear rub from James. When James was ready, all three of us went together down the stairs.

"I had a great time today, Cheryl. Thank you. I'm feeling different."

"You're welcome sweets, and you *are* different. But, same assignment; to make contact next week on the couch and see if you can do it without my help, okay? You're making great progress and it's all coming together. You just need to keep practicing."

I gave him a quick, final hug. "See you next week. Have a good one."

And with that, Sammy the cat and I saw him out the door and onto the walk. He walked past the edge of the doorway with a little wave of the hand, and headed out of sight down the walk.

I removed my "session in progress" sign from the door and went to the phone to give my report to Dr Johnston.

CHAPTER 14
TAKING TIME, THE HIDDEN LOVER, SOME PRESENTING ISSUES

.

A few clients, not many, have a suppressed talent for intimacy like James, a sort of innate sense of the many facets of sexuality. This is the secret or hidden lover. At some point in our work together, he comes out in small ways: a knowing look in the eye, a raised eyebrow or perhaps a smoky, teasing voice. At first, his excursions out are in small flashes that I recognize, especially from my own response to them, that little thrill in my body that says I'm being seduced. There is an intention of seduction that I feel.

As we work through the process and the client becomes more comfortable with himself and his sexuality, the hidden lover feels more permission to express himself and his time out becomes longer and longer. This happens as a result of the normalizing of sex, of making it natural and healthy, robust and free. We do this with insight, sharing, laughter and caring, spiced with dash of daring.

Unfortunately, many clients, though able to get to the point of normal sexual functioning at least, are unable to access their natural, free sensual self. In those cases, I have to trust that should they find a relationship, it will be the right one for them that will support their level of development and that with time and practice some of that will come forward. But even if they never venture into relationship, just feeling better about themselves, and more confident, generally changes the way they interact with the world.

Some cases that I deal with are fairly technical. Premature ejaculation, though it often has psychological or emotional causes, such as getting it over with or being too close or too vulnerable, for example, doesn't always require deep introspection. It can be caused by the simple act of having created a signature, a pattern of going for the gold, doing it solely for the orgasm. These patterns are usually established in puberty and reinforced throughout life in masturbation.

The technique of teaching a client where his own personal pleasure meter number 6 or 7 is on a scale of one to ten, where 10 is the orgasm, can make it easier to prevent early ejaculation. If he can learn to ride the wave at a 7 by changing techniques, slowing down or changing focus, he can prolong his orgasm until he chooses to come, rather than being the victim of "too soon" orgasms.

Fortunately, along the way he'll also learn the delights of going slowly and that *all* the pleasurable things people do to each other before coming is "having sex." Coming needs to be the gravy, the dessert, the goodies, not the only course of what could be a sumptuous meal.

Erectile dysfunction can be a physical or emotional issue and can be a combination of both. Some ED is due to age or physical complications and some to anxiety, fear or other emotional components. For a client with normal functioning during masturbation, relaxation, time to allow arousal to build, learning to enjoy the whole of sexuality, rather than just intercourse, is the goal. Viagra has certainly helped, but in my experience, as I've said earlier, if there is little or no libido, it doesn't help a lot.

For men unable, because of physical issues, to ever achieve erections, there are a variety of options besides medication: Injections, external pumps to engorge the penis and in severe cases surgical implants, which seem to have been fairly successful. Research and consultations with one's doctor can provide the best option for each individual.

For less severe cases, cock rings, tightly placed at the base of the penis trapping the blood, can aid in creating and sustaining an erection. Even for those with no difficulties in this area using a cock ring can add a little spice to the moment and actually help in those times when you want to have sex and things just aren't working.

Some clients have social phobias, in which case a lot of work needs to be done to lessen the fear around interaction both socially and intimately.

Virgins, if we limit it to intercourse, range anywhere from late twenties to my oldest at seventy-five and come to the work with a variety of reasons for the lack of experience.

In all the above cases, learning how to experience sensation, through sensate focus, is the beginning.

Those who are physically challenged are another type of client. In the case of a severely disabled person, the work might be to help them find the erogenous zones on some part of the body that they *can* feel, or to assist them in finding ways that they can sexually please their partner.

In the slightly less disabled it might be finding positions that work for their body or determining how much help they need to get into that position and how to achieve pleasure once there. The fact that a client is disabled does not necessarily mean that they are incapable of experiencing sensation or of sustaining erections.

I know that some disabled clients of surrogates have been able to find and sustain loving relationships after their time in therapy. But again, sometimes the healing is simply in the process of being touched and held.

Beyond physical and emotional issues, there are clients with sexual fetishes who need help to overcome their feelings of embarrassment or weirdness about their preferences, to accept that it is okay and to know that there are others out there that will share their enjoyment.

I once went to an erotic boutique and bought a pair of sexy panty hose for a young male client doing an intensive two-week course of therapy with me. It had taken halfway through the process for him to get to a place where he felt comfortable telling me and it only came about because I was wearing a pair that day and he expressed an interest in how they would feel and wanted to try them on. They didn't fit of course, resulting in my purchase of a pair large enough for a man.

In my practice, the term of my own work to completion with a client is very seldom less than 10 sessions and can sometimes continue on for a year or so to complete treatment. If the client is a virgin, my preference is to see them well into dating and in some cases, the beginning of a relationship, if that is what they are seeking.

Sexual and intimate discomfort comes with many different faces and causes and it takes time and trust to relax, get comfortable, heal the causes of discomfort, and to be able to tolerate the intimacy itself.

CHAPTER 15
JAMES

I opened the door the following week to a smiling James. He seemed in a good mood when he gave me a hug in the entranceway. It was a cold, windy day and his slightly ruffled hair and pink cheeks told me he'd been out in it awhile, and his jacket felt cool through my shirt.

"Have you been waiting outside?" I asked, "You look cold."

"No, not waiting. I did get here early, so I took a walk through the neighborhood to kill some time. It is cold outside, though. But, it feels good in here."

"Yes, it feels like a curl up in front of the fire kind of day. Let me hang up your jacket," I said, taking it from him and placing it on the back of a dining room chair. "So, did you have your coffee date?"

"Yeah, I did. It went pretty well. It was good, I think, but let me use the bathroom and then I'll tell you all about it."

"Okay, I'll be on the couch."

He went into the bathroom and I wandered into the living room, stopping to pet Sammy, who had come to give his usual greeting. I picked up one of the glasses of water I had waiting on the glass coffee table and sat down and sipped at it while I waited. I was eager to hear his news. It would be great if he could at least begin to date while we proceeded with our work. He was coming along nicely, and barring any more little glitches, would be able to make it through at least the basics before long, and if we could coax the secret lover man in him out more, I felt he'd do fine. Time to add a little more eroticism. I had been giving thought to inviting him to a sensual shower.

James emerged from the bathroom and also stopped to say hello and give a scratch behind the ears to Sammy, who had been waiting for him at the hallway entrance to the bathroom. "How you doin' old man? You're lookin' good!" He greeted the greeter and joined me on the couch.

"Well, tell me!" I said as he sat down.

"Well, there's not too much to tell yet. She's even prettier than her picture and she's got a nice enough body. Kind of big breasts, I think, which I like, like yours," he smiled and raised his eyebrows.

"Well, thank you." I smiled in return and got him back on track. "What did you talk about?"

"We told each other about our work and she told me she's been married and had a couple of fairly long term relationships. All I said was that I've been concentrating more on my work than on relationships, which is true, but now that I feel like I've sort of got it together work wise, I'm interested in finding one." He shrugged, looking at me for reassurance and I nodded in return.

"Anyway, we talked for about an hour and a half and she asked me to call her, so I guess she thinks I'm okay. I'll probably call her this week and maybe go to a movie or dinner or something. But maybe you could help me with what to say about why I don't have much experience."

"Well, just remember, that when we finish, you will have experience, and we do have a relationship, after all. It's just different, but no one needs to know that, right?"

James responded with a tilt of his head and a shrug. "No, I guess not."

"You don't have to disclose that you've only had one. Like you said, maybe you've been busy getting your professional career together and haven't made time for a long-term relationship. When you do have one, a relationship with someone, you may or may not consider divulging more, but until then I don't think that you need to tell everyone about your situation. Anyway, we'll be talking more about it as we go along, as things come up I'm sure, but for now, how are you feeling about all of this? Our work, I mean."

"Really good, I think! I'm feeling more confident about myself and being with you is really helping. You know, after I got home and thought about it, last time was awesome! I did something I never thought I'd want to do and I think I'd be able to do it again. I felt different when I left."

"Great! That makes me really happy and if you want to do it again, you won't get any complaints from me!"

"Okay, but know what? Right now, I'd like to kiss you, if that's okay?" He moved a little closer to put his arm around me.

"Absolutely!" I replied, hearing that my voice sounded rather sultry, and turned toward him.

He put both his arms around me and we began what turned out to be a ten minute or so, quite stimulating, make-out session. Since the erotic shower idea still ran through my mind, it felt like a perfect intro.

"Hey, I have an idea," I said pulling away a bit. "How about a nice shower?"

"A shower? Uh-oh, do I have a problem? I mean, I showered this morning." He sniffed suspiciously at his armpit.

I thought he must be teasing, but wasn't sure. "Oh, no," I laughed, I don't mean a shower to get clean, I mean a shower to have fun."

"Oh. Well, okay, I guess. Sure, sounds like it might be fun. I've seen it in movies, but I've never done it."

His tone was as enthusiastic as I would have wanted. "Well, there's a lot of things you haven't done before that are fun. And more to come."

This time I got up from the couch and offered him my hand. "Let's go get wet then, times' a-wastin," and I led him upstairs.

At my suggestion, James went ahead into our room to remove his clothes, while I stepped into my lavender walled bathroom to start the shower. Once the hot water flowed into the tub, I adjusted it to be fairly hot, enough to make steam, to help us along. There's just something about a steamy shower!

James came in trying to look casual and stood watching me as I quickly took off my own clothes. Taking his hand again, I stepped behind the beige shower curtain, pulling him with me and we took turns letting the water run down our bodies.

I turned him away from me and I began first, pouring the scented liquid soap onto his shoulders and using my hands to make circles of suds across his back and down and under his arms.

Rivers of bubbles slipped down his body and I rubbed my body against his as I followed the stream down to the crack of his ass and down his thighs. Pressing against him, I reached around his body, soaping his chest and stroking his stiffening cock.

He turned and put his hands on my waist and pulled me to him, kissing my neck. "Can I have some soap too?"

I handed him the bottle and he poured some into his hand and sharing it with his other hand, he took my breasts in his palms. He massaged them, making them slippery with bubbles and my nipples responded, stimulated by the movement of his hand and the slight sting of the hot water. He used more soap and stroked his hand down my belly and between my legs and finally, pressing his body to mine, kissed me, pushing me back against the shower wall.

We did a lot more kissing and rubbing and sliding off one another, stroking each other all over until finally, both of us, feeling hot and slightly drowned, decided it was time to get out. If we were further along in our work, it would have been fun to have sex in the shower, but we hadn't gotten there yet. He was a good shower partner though, getting into the fun and the eroticism of it.

We dried one another with my burgundy towels and I wiped off the mirror and did my best with a brush to make some sense of my hair. James had already gone to our room again and when I entered he lay on the bed, with the creamy blanket draped casually across his lower half, smiling. "Now, that was fun!"

I climbed onto the bed and he threw the blanket across me and I welcomed the coziness. The air in the room felt cool, after the hot shower.

Facing me, James draped one arm across me. "You know, I was turned on enough that I think I could have had intercourse with you in there."

His arm felt heavy and warm. Raising my eyebrows I teased, "I know, I could sort of tell," as I reached down and patted his now only slightly erect cock, "but we're not quite there, yet. It's important also, to be able to just have sensual fun, just fun, and if intercourse is a part of it then all the more fun. Just being in the moment, in pleasure, makes us relax and gives us confidence about our bodies. So we're getting there, you know?"

"Yeah, yeah, I know, and it 's all great, really. I can wait. I really want to be good at all this and this is all good stuff." His hand had slipped into action and softly stroked my backside.

So, what do you think you'd like to do with the rest of our time today?"

"Well, maybe I could pick up where we left off last time. I'd like to see some more of what you like."

"That's fine with me! Do you need anything?" I asked.

"Nope, just your body…and you, of course." He leaned over me and began kissing me and my body, and this time with a lot less tentativeness. He worked his way down and once he got to my pussy, he experimented with different touches and finally brought his mouth into play. He asked if I liked different things that he did and remembering his previous lesson, asked me what I might like more.

This time I felt more able to relax and just enjoy it, which, in turn, seemed to inspire him, so he spent enough time and did enough of what I really like, to inspire a very sweet orgasm for me. Once it had subsided, I looked down at James, who had stopped what he was doing and was looking back at me and smiling like a kid at Christmas.

"You sounded like you liked that!" He was grinning like a goofy fool.

"Um, yep, those sounds were me I'm afraid. That was nice!" I sighed.

"It was great! I loved it! It was a real turn on, watching you."

He still looked so pleased with himself that I actually giggled, but got myself together. "Come on up here and let's cuddle for awhile. That would feel really nice to me after that."

He crawled up beside me and put his arms around me, kissing me on the shoulder. And the state of his cock told me he was still turned on, but I knew that we were running short on time, so we would have to let that go for another session.

James, basking in his self-satisfied state, seemed fine with just cuddling for a bit.

"You know", he said thoughtfully, "most of the time that I was doing it, I didn't have a hard on, but when you started to make noise like you were coming, all of a sudden I got turned on."

"Yeah, that happens sometimes. Maybe you're absorbed in what you're doing, or thinking about what you're doing, so you're not in your own arousal, but as you can see, it's not really a problem, is it?" I reached down and stroked his dick lightly.

He laughed. "No, I guess not and that's reassuring, to say the least. I think I'm starting to worry less about that. My dick seems to be behaving pretty well."

"Good. It's mostly relaxing, enjoying yourself and not watching it all the time. And, letting the arousal build, of course."

We lay together for our last five minutes, just talking quietly and laughing, feeling cozy and comfortable with each other and when we had to get up to get dressed, there was a little melancholy in the air between us. Sometimes it's hard to cut off the closeness and re-enter the outer world.

We exchanged another warm hug at the door as I saw him out. This had been an important session for James. It's an amazing thing to share someone's pleasure and my orgasm had been his first experience with that.

I was sure it must have been empowering.

CHAPTER 16
JAMES

Over the next few sessions, James and I remained at about the same level, practicing things we'd already done. He always had the assignment to begin contact with me, so we spent a good amount of time on the couch, working our way up from first date material, like conversation and how much of himself he wanted to share, to more intimate engagements, with kissing and fondling and making the segue to the bedroom.

Once there we had more fun with manual play and oral sex, always aiming at greater relaxation and more ease of communication for James. He had his first orgasm with me during oral sex after a sustained period of arousal. An orgasm seems as though it should

196

be natural and easy, but sometimes tension makes it hard to accomplish. In my work it can express a level of comfort and trust and is sometimes cause for a small celebration.

Of course, in men with rapid ejaculation problems, we are working the other way, finding levels at which to sustain, without orgasm. Longer stimulation and no orgasm would be cause for celebration in those circumstances, too.

During this time James had little problem with loss of erections. The level of play we were engaged in had kept arousal in a heightened state for extended periods of time, and we had not yet approached the area of intercourse, where James had had his experiences of failure.

Outside the bedroom, in James' world, he had had a couple of dates with the first woman he connected with through the dating service and anticipated meeting with a few more, but so far, aside from some easy kissing, no real activity. He was really moving ahead in the dating area. His self- confidence continued to improve, but his issues around intercourse needed to be dealt with before he could let himself get that close. For him, it felt like too much risk, even though he had been easily sustaining arousal in our time together.

We had been drawing closer, talking about many different aspects of our lives. Really getting to know each other, becoming friends as well as sexual partners and finally, it felt that we were at a place to move forward.

In my practice, this first venture into intercourse is with what we call "quiet penetration." It's an opportunity to have successful penetration, without the pressure of performing. In fact, the idea is to penetrate and become still, allowing the erection to diminish, while staying connected.

The ultimate purpose is to discover that one can lose an erection and get it back again, taking the anxiety out of the idea of intercourse, but in the beginning it's simply to learn to be okay with losing it and not feeling that it makes one a failure. Also, importantly, to have some experience with what to do if it does happen.

Sometimes I discuss it with a client ahead of time and sometimes not and in James case, I had decided to sort of just let it happen in the moment. He still had enough anxiety around the whole thing that it seemed the better idea.

Just making genital-to-genital contact is the first step and if that feels comfortable to the client we could proceed to penetration.

In our current session, James and I had been enjoying one another for awhile, stroking and touching, and his arousal had sustained a nice erection so it seemed like it might be the time to introduce it. Since he already had a condom on, I suggested that he get on top of me between my legs and just lay with me.

He agreed and carefully moved his body to lay on me with his elbows propped at the side. "Is this okay," he asked. "Am I too heavy?"

"Huh-uh, it's fine," I assured him.

He moved his hips a little and I could feel his cock nudging me as if it was seeking entrance. I let that go on for a few minutes and then asked "How does this feel to you? Are you comfortable with this kind of contact?"

"Yeah, it feels nice. I like it." He was silent for a few moments, his head nestled by my neck. He pressed his hips against me with his cock caught between us. Then he said, "You know, I think I'm ready for more."

"Does that mean that you'd like to come in, James?" I said softly in his ear.

"Yeah, I think so. Would it be okay?""

"Yes, it's okay, so why don't you back up just a little and let me guide you," I suggested.

As he pulled back I took hold of his penis and guided him in. This, for me, is a better approach for the first time, than letting him fumble around, or having it take so long so that he loses his erection and gets discouraged before we even get started.

James was looking at me with some concern in his brown eyes, the furrow between them showing his tension. I knew he was cock watching, trying to determine whether it was staying or going, so I put my arms around him and drew him close and murmured in his ear, "You don't need to move, sweetie, we're going to just lay here and let it go. There's nothing you need to do, except just relax."

"Really?" He sounded doubtful.

"Yep. It'll be okay. It's just the first step, trust me." I stroked his back to distract him slightly.

"Okay," he said. "I'd really like to do more, but I'll try to relax."

Not doing more right now was the ideal thing, because I could feel his erection waning as we spoke. So, we became quiet and held one another for about ten minutes, until the feeling of his slipping out became too uncomfortable and we parted ways to simply lie side-by- side looking at one another.

"Sooo, why did we do it like that?" he asked, sounding confused.

"So that you can see that all is not lost, if your hard on deserts you. I'll bet you a dollar we can get it back," I teased, and with that, I reached down and began stroking him. He had a slow response, due of course to his anxiety, but with some time, various kinds of attention, and a light hearted atmosphere, he was quite ready for anything.

Some clients might need to remain at this step of quiet penetration and re-stimulating for some time, building trust and confidence. The next step would be to have penetration, let it go and see if we could stimulate interest again, while he remained inside.

Depending on the client this can take awhile, because the instinct to watch, at first, is difficult to overcome. Because of that, I decided that it would be best to save any more intercourse for the next session, as I didn't want to take the chance on James' leaving this session feeling discouraged. That might happen in the future, but today we had a good start at his gaining some confidence in his penis, so we spent the rest of our session together with James practicing putting on condoms quickly.

It was fun, if a bit frustrating for him, but I wouldn't have been surprised to learn that being slow at it and feeling clumsy contributed to his erection difficulties in intercourse. It's a common thing to have happen and the antidote for it is to practice, practice, practice, until one could do it in the dark or with their eyes closed. I've known men that could snap them on in seconds and be ready to pounce with fervor.

Like I always say, "Remember, the condom is your friend!" so, this session, I sent James off with instructions to buy an extra box for his homework.

CHAPTER 17
THE VISIT

It was at this point in our work together that James and I agreed that one of our sessions would involve my making a trip to his condo to determine whether it was currently female ready, a place to which he would feel comfortable bringing a date and where she would feel welcomed.

I have visited client's apartments in the past with mixed experiences. Some were presentable and others reflected the clients sense of isolation: Clothes on the floor (even when they knew I'd be coming), bathrooms that could stand a cleaning, and beds that looked as though a caveman had been sleeping there, with various bits of food wrappers lying around, a number of glasses that never made it back to the kitchen and piles of mail or papers here and there in various places in the living room.

Some would make an effort to clean up in preparation for my visit, but even with that, evidence of their style of living remained: Things not quite clean and the scent of never opened windows hanging about in the air.

Conversely, I had one client whose perfectionism had trapped him in a loveless life, and that need for perfection and control was reflected in his home; everything in its proper place, spotlessly clean and with little color or style. He had created a sterile environment, with no touches of warmth, no reflection of the person who lived there and actually no feeling that *anyone* lived there. As he grew and changed, we talked about things like adding colored pillows on the couch and pictures on the wall.

I never saw his apartment again, but from his reports of improvements he'd made, I was pretty sure that it must be at least warmer and more comfortable looking. All the improvements he'd implemented were in small things that he felt he could control. I don't know if he actually ever entertained there, but he seemed happy and content with his newly comfortable surroundings and felt that he could invite women home if he wished, and make them feel at home.

I've told my clients that women certainly don't expect a man's apartment necessarily look like the way theirs does, but we do expect it to be clean and cared for. A rumpled apartment might be good for a night or two, if things are hot, but the good will about it wouldn't last long. Grown women expect grown men to have some care about how they live.

When James opened the door of his apartment, the following Thursday, his smile was warm and said he was happy to see me, but I knew him well enough by now to detect the signs of his nervousness; his body moved too quickly and with an awkwardness as he swung the door back and stepped to the side to allow me entry.

As I entered, the feeling I had on the first glance at his apartment was much the same as he seemed when I met him at my door the first time, no frills, nothing fancy, but clean and well taken care of. It was actually quite presentable, but certainly didn't reflect the man I saw him becoming.

Presentable would do of course, but I was interested in seeing how he felt about it now. Were there things he might like to change? I'm not an interior designer and I've never expected my own men to be design conscious, but it's delightful to see some expression of a person in their home, whether it's a man or a woman.

James' living room was neat and the couch comfortable. I leaned back into the overstuffed cushions and happily accepted his offer of tea.

As he disappeared into the kitchen, to prepare it, I had a good look around. It was pretty generic, including the few poster pictures on the wall of sports cars and a street scene of what could have been almost any European city. A large flat-screen TV occupied another wall and something that looked like a sound system filled the low console beneath it. A square coffee table, a couple of end tables and lamps that looked like they had come from a hotel furniture warehouse store and that was it. Not bad, not good......generic.

"May I take a look at the bedroom?" I asked, getting up and starting down the hall toward the room that I knew must be in that direction.

"Sure," he called, "It's the second door down. The first one is the office."

The first thing I saw and which anyone coming back with him for sex would see, was the bed. A fairly neatly made, nondescript, plain, greenish colored spread over a king size mattress. Utilitarian, but hardly spoke of a man who thought he might entertain here, or of the sexy man beginning to creep out in James's and my sessions.

My first purpose in coming here; simply to see if his place would be fit for bringing someone home with him, was satisfied. Cleanliness is the most important thing. But, because James had come to a point where his life was changing and opening, I myself felt interested in seeing how that might apply here, where he lived.

Because I had already gotten a pretty good idea of his living conditions I just took a quick peek into his office, which looked like any other office, with the usual office items arranged around the small room. It consisted of a desk and chair, a computer, file cabinet and some messiness on the desk. No big deal.

Then, as I heard sounds of James returning to the living room, I took a look in the bathroom. The seat of the toilet was up, of course, to be expected, which gave me a chance to see how clean it was. It seemed fairly clean, but as I stood there, the faint scent of urine, punctured my nose.

James, like some men I've observed, clean the center of the toilet, but not around the rim or the outside and often not the floor around the toilet. They seem to forget that when you're standing up, urine splashes. Maybe because they don't sit down as much, or maybe because they're just oblivious to the smell, they don't realize it, but this woman's nose (and I know my nose is not alone) can smell it and it's a big turn off! If all I can think about is cleaning the toilet, I'm hardly going to be thinking about having sex! Joking aside, it was only one small demerit mark for his home.

"So, what do you think?" James asked. He sat on the edge of the sofa, with his mug of tea in front of him and as I sat down to join him, the scent of peppermint drifted up from my own to greet me.

"Not bad. Did you clean before I came?" I asked, fairly sure of the answer.

"Of course. Wasn't I supposed to?"

"Well sure, I certainly appreciate it, but how bad do you think it was, before you cleaned, on a scale of one to ten? Because you may not always know when you might bring someone home, so it's good to keep an eye on it and keep it under control."

"Yeah, I know," he admitted sheepishly.

"I'd say it was at least a six, at least on my scale. The thing is, when I'm home, I'm mostly in the office, so it can get messed up, but since I don't spend a lot of time out here in the living room, mostly just to watch TV, I really don't think about it. I keep the kitchen pretty clean though. One good thing my mother instilled in me, I guess."

Some sarcasm colored the last sentence. By now, we had determined that his mother had been pretty intrusive when he was growing up, not respecting his privacy, snooping in his room and prying into every area of his life.

He harbored a lot of anger about that. Interestingly, it didn't present itself much in our work together, but he and Dr. Johnston had spent a good deal of time on it in their sessions. Consequently, he had made good progress in separating his mother from not only me, but also women with whom he might establish relationships. However, if he actually lived with someone, it certainly could present itself in circumstances of the privacy issues that might come up when you share space with another.

"James, were you alright with me snooping around?" I asked, after a sip of tea.

"Oh, it's fine. I knew you were coming and why you were coming and I know you're only trying to help me. I was nervous before you got here though. Afraid I wouldn't pass inspection, I guess." He looked around the room for a moment.

"I guess it's kind of plain, huh? Compared to your place, anyway. Your place is really nice."

"Well, thanks, but yours is fine for a bachelor's pad. It could use a few more touches of your self, but otherwise, not bad. It seems clean and well kept and you know, women don't expect a lot from a single man's place." I smiled.

"Remember, that my place has had my feminine touch. We're generally the ones that do the nesting, bringing in things that warm up a home. The only thing I would suggest in your surroundings, is that you could have a few things that reflect your interests and give your surroundings more color, more personal texture. I see from your posters that you seem to like sports cars?"

"Yeah, pretty much. I'd like to own a Porsche someday."

"Good then, the posters tell me something about you. Do you think the colors in your place are colors you really like? Like your bedspread? Do you like that color?" I felt like the tone of my voice and the expression on my face might have been reflecting my own feelings of ho-hum about it.

James laughed, "I guess you don't," and laughed again.

"No, not particularly." I admitted, laughing myself.

"Damn! Busted!" James exclaimed. "Actually, someone gave it to me and it looked better than the one I had so I used it. It covered the bed and so it worked for me. But, maybe I should get something different."

"I just think that it would be nice to have some color in your room. You know, a comforter or something that's a color you really like. All I'm saying is that your place looks okay, but it could use a little more of what makes you feel good to be here. Just think about it. Anyway, just as it is, it's perfectly fine to bring a woman home to. Better than a lot of men's places, for sure. There is one thing though, that needs some work."

The little smile created by my approval rating disappeared and his forehead turned into a crease of concern. "Really? What's that?"

"The toilet."

"The toilet?"

"Mm-hmm."

"But, I'm sure I cleaned it. Didn't I? I don't think I was in there afterward……Oh no, was there something in there?" He laid back against the couch pillows, his hand on his forehead.

"No, no, it's not that." I had to laugh at his discomfort. Funny, how uptight we all get about anyone seeing the results of our personal food disposal. I heard a sigh of relief from him.

"It's just that you need to clean the rim, around the edges and especially on the floor. When I stood in there, I could smell urine and it's a turn off, which you definitely don't want."

"Oh damn, I'm sorry." Chagrin covered his face.

"No need to apologize to me. That's what I'm here for, after all." I took a sip of my cooling tea.

"All in all, I give your place three stars. A clean toilet, a little more color and you're definitely in the four star category. For a straight bachelor." I laughed and patted him on the thigh.

He laughed a little too at my "straight bachelor" remark, then took my hand and held it. "Thanks Cheryl. I'll think about what you said and make sure the john doesn't smell. I didn't really smell it myself, so I'll take your woman's word for it." He smiled again and let go of my hand, leaned forward and picked up his own mug.

We had agreed that my travel time would be included in our session, so it was getting close to the end of time together for this week. We sat for a few minutes chatting about my drive over in traffic and the weather report for the next few days as we finished our tea.

"Well, I think I'd better be going. I don't want to run into rush hour traffic and my timing should be good right now. Thank you for the tea James. So I'll see you next week, at my place?" I stood and picked up my purse from the couch.

"Absolutely, and thanks again for coming over. I see what you mean about color and stuff. I think it just takes a little thinking about what I like, instead of just having a place to eat and sleep."

He walked with me to the door and gave me a warm hug and we shared a goodbye kiss.

"See you later, coach. Drive safe."

"Thanks, I will. See you next week." Another small peck on the lips and I went on my way.

CHAPTER 18

JAMES MEETS JENNIFER

At our next meeting, James reported that he had continued making dates with various women and that one had gone really well. Her name was Jennifer. They met for coffee and ended up talking for two hours. Although he thought she talked quite a bit, maybe out of nerves he said, he had found her very pretty, with an attractive body, and importantly, she seemed interested in him, enough to take the initiative and kiss him at the end. He told her that he would call her and she seemed happy about it.

"I'm not rushing anything right now, but I'll call her and maybe have dinner or something. I'll just see how it goes the second time."

"That sounds good. In the meantime, we have more work to do, but you're really doing well, don't you think?"

"Yeah, I'm beginning to realize how far I've come, since we all started working together. You know, I've been thinking though, if I'm going to actually have a date with Jennifer, I don't know how to handle myself with a woman, like holding her hand or other things people do on a date."

"Well, do you want to practice it? We could do that here."

"Yeah, that'd be great! Just to give me some idea of how to get started."

"Okay," I got up from the couch. "Let's take a walk around the living room."

James joined me and we spent the next fifteen minutes walking back and forth and around, practicing different ways for him to make first walking contact, placing his hand gently on her back to sort of usher her through a door, how to take her hand, without looking or feeling too awkward, or putting his arm around her. He did pretty well, but of course it would take some practice and more importantly, some sense of comfort with the person he was with. When we were finished we sat and relaxed back on the couch.

"So, did that help a bit? How was that for you?" I asked.

"It felt kind of awkward, but I know it's going to feel weird the first few times. Maybe we could practice some more, later. At least I have an idea of how to get started." He paused and looked at me for a long moment and I was surprised by the little gleam I swear I saw in his eye.

"But you know, now I'd like to get going on all the other stuff we still have to do." He smiled a funny, crooked little smile that I found endearingly sexy, and he reached over and took my hand. He held it for a minute, looked at me and pulled me closer for a kiss.

Oh, there were changes all right! While it may have been a little boost of confidence that he received on his last date, I'm sure that in his previous unsuccessful experiences the women were interested too. The difference now, was that he had begun to feel that he might be able to handle the situation and even just that would open a door in him for the sexual James to step through.

Not only able to make the moves, he was also learning to connect, something that had been happening quietly, underneath the external work. So far, this was with me, someone with whom he felt comfortable, and the trick now would be to make it solid, so that he could call on these resources when with another woman.

More confidence and continuing practice would take him a long way toward being able to take advantage of spontaneous sexuality, like hot, first date connections, as well as more intimate lovemaking opportunities. We were getting there, but we still had a ways to go.

We stayed on the couch for a while, lying back, kissing, pressing our bodies together and touching. Finally, James's knee was between my legs and the feeling of not being able to get close enough was building between us, so I suggested that we take our party upstairs.

Once in the bedroom, James, suddenly a little awkward, put his arms around me and held me for a moment.

"You seem a little uncomfortable," I asked, "is everything alright?"

"Yeah, yeah, I'm fine. It's just that sometimes making the shift from there to here feels, I don't know, kind of weird."

"Yeah, I know what you mean. But, you know, I think it's probably just the stage we're at. You know, we get all hot and then we have to slow it down, so it feels kind of disconnected. But, if that's it, and I think it is, it'll get better when you have all your options available, when we can just move into having sex, having fun. Besides, I think you're anticipating a little, don't you?"

"Yeah, probably more than a little. I've been thinking about it a lot and now that it's here again, I'm nervous," he admitted.

"Well, try to calm yourself. There's really no pressure for you to do anything. We don't have to continue with intercourse today and even if we do, there's no requirement for you to do it just right. If we get to that, it'll be different again, than you might expect. We're just going to play with the whole thing, so you can get an idea of what your body's really like, what it needs and what works for you. It's fine. Just relax. You and your dick are in friendly territory."

James smiled and even laughed, just a bit. "Okay, I'll,.. uh, I'll do my best."

"Just breathe, alright? And get your clothes off right now," I ordered with mock sternness, as I began taking my own off. "I'll be waiting for you in bed."

I hurried to beat him to nakedness, flipped the music on, and jumped onto the bed. I covered myself with the blanket and poised on one side, with my hand supporting my head, and watched him as he finished taking his clothes off and laying them on the chair.

"You look ready, so here I come!" He jumped in beside me and pulled the blanket over himself. He lay down on his side facing me and we wrapped our arms around each other. "Oh yeah," he sighed, "This is good."

We cuddled like that for a while, running our hands softly over one another's body, feeling each other's skin, while we talked about not much of anything. The kind of talk that you can't usually remember later, more murmurs than anything substantial. After a bit, James' touches became hungry as he caressed my breasts, hips and thighs.

"I really love your body...a dancer's body. It feels strong, but soft."

"Thank you, I'm glad you like it. I like yours too, and you do have a very handsome cock, which hmmm, seems to be pretty interested in what we're doing," I teased. As I stroked it, his erection became stronger, so I decided again to take the bull by the horns, so to speak, and reached over for a condom.

"Do you want to do this James, or shall I?"

"No, I'll do it. Can't let all that practice go to waste." He laid back and actually got it on pretty quickly. Fast enough so that his erection didn't visibly wane. I love clients that do their homework! It really pays off, in all areas.

"Do you mind if I take over?' I asked, already rolling over onto him. I hoped my light and teasing tone would allay any feelings of anxiety. I knelt above him, my knees on either side of his hips.

I reached down and took hold of his cock and said "Here hold this, with me." He reached down and held it firmly in place.

"Now let me do the work, for now, okay?" And with that I placed myself in alignment and lowered myself onto him. He put his hands on my hips and watched me as I moved and increasingly there was response from his pelvis, until we were moving together. His eyes were wide, but he was grinning. I gave it a minute and then asked, "How're you doing, James?"

"I'm doin' great! This is great. You're great!" His voice held a sense of wonder, mixed with excitement.

"Um-hum it does feel good. But I hope you'll still think I'm great, because I'm going to stay here, but I'm going to stop moving."

"Why?" He looked dismayed.

"Everything's fine, but I want to let your hard-on go down."

"But, we did that last time. I thought this time we were going go all the way," he complained, looking disgruntled.

I explained, "Well, we might, but it's important for you right now to be able to know that you can get your erection back, if it goes, and how to get it back. So my plan is to let it go, get it back and play some more."

"But what if it doesn't come back?" He said anxiously.

"We'll find a way. Your body's way. We'll work to-gether. If it came up once, it can come up again, so relax, if you can, and just be with me."

"Okay, I guess you're the boss. So, what do we do?" He was biting his lip.

"Nothing, I'm just going to lay down on you." Careful to keep him inside me, I laid on top of his chest, my chin resting in the side of his neck.

"Is this comfortable for you?" I asked.

His hands were hot and roaming my body, caressing my butt. "Yeah, you feel nice."

"Hey, you!" I rose up a bit. "Just relax and hold me. We'll get back to the butt and stuff later. We're supposed to let it go, remember?" Actually, with all the consternation on his part, his erection had already gone down somewhat and I didn't want to let it get too far, so we had to pay attention.

He smiled a little sheepishly, "Okay, okay, I'll try to be good."

As we lay together, I could tell from the slight tension in his body that he was aware and anxiously watching his erection. It's a built in reaction, something most men are afraid of happening, so I would have been surprised if he didn't. But we were doing this so that he could allay some of his fears by learning that erection loss doesn't have to mean the end of everything.

This was where he had suffered the feelings of humiliation that had deeply impacted his personal life, so for James this was an extremely important part of our work, and I knew that for him it felt dangerous.

When I felt that we were close to losing our connection I sat up and began moving a little again. He was definitely soft, so I moved carefully, not enough to lose him, but to gently stimulate, rubbing rather than rising.

The furrow was back between his eyebrows and his brown eyes looked back at me with concern. "I'm pretty soft, I don't know if this is going to work."

"Don't think about that right now, James, it doesn't matter at the moment, just focus on the sensations. Touch me."

I took his hands and guided them to my breasts. "Focus on the things that feel good. If it doesn't happen now, we have other things to do, so just be with what your hands and body are feeling." I paused for a few moments to give him a chance to do that.

I looked down at his frowning face. "Try to think of this as fun, James. Imagine all the other dull things you could be doing right now. Isn't this much better, whatever happens? It sure is for me," I laughed, "Hey, I could be doing dishes or something. This is much more fun and you feel good, soft or not."

I wasn't lying. For me, the warm, fat feeling of a soft or semi erect cock can be quite pleasurable; different, but pleasurable.

"Yeah, I could be sweating over a hot computer instead, right now, I guess," he said, smiling just a little.

His hands were beginning to move of their own accord so I asked him to put some energy into his pelvis, to move with me a little bit, which he did. After a few minutes of this, we began to get some response from his penis; a chubby, semi-erect. This was a good sign, because when he really relaxed, he might easily go to full erection, just doing this.

"Am I getting hard? I can't really tell." James asked.

"Well, it feels like you're on the way, but we're not supposed to be cock watching," I answered. "Let's just play. Relax. We'll see what happens. No pressure, alright?"

"Yeah, okay, maybe. It helps for me to move some, because otherwise I can't feel a lot. Is that normal?"

'Yes," I responded, "it is and I can tell you why, but not right now. All this talk is taking the magic away and I can tell you're starting to worry, so if you don't mind, let's stop for now. We can come back to this in a bit."

As I got off and cuddled up to him, he lifted his arm, laid his forearm across his forehead and sighed, a sign I interpreted as frustration.

"Hey," I put my hand on his chest and patted it lightly, the hairs tickling my wrist, "don't go there. We're not done yet. We've got some time and I intend to use it."

James lowered his arm and put it around me. "Sorry. Yeah, I can't seem to get out of my head."

"In answer to your question about not feeling much, the reason you're not is because you're used to much firmer pressure with masturbation. Right?"

James nodded, "Yeah, seems like it."

"Well, the vagina is a far more subtle feeling and it takes a little more focus at first and paying attention to what you can feel. Sometimes a little imagery helps, paying attention to the visuals or sounds or just getting off on the idea of what you're doing, what you want to do. You know, imagining that feeling of 'Yeah, baby, I'm gonna do you.' It also keeps you from thinking too much. I don't want to talk more right now, but when we're done, help me remember some homework to give you about your masturbation."

James nodded and turned more toward me. "So what now?"

"Well, what would you like? What do you think would feel really good?"

'Umm," hesitating, he pressed his lips together and looked at me with raised eyebrows "maybe some head?"

It made me laugh, the way he looked, all naughty school-boy, as he asked.

"Okay, I'm happy to oblige," I said and began moving down his body.

I put my mouth on his soft cock and after a couple of minutes I began hearing soft sounds of pleasure from him. As I added the use of my hand with what I was doing, his cock began to respond. Ah, the pleasures of oral sex. It almost always works.

I continued until his erection was in full arousal and then said, "Would you like to get on top of *me*, this time?" I thought that maybe he'd have more control over stimulation by being able to move more.

He sat up. "Okay, maybe that'll be better right now."

I put a pillow under my hips to give him more access. As he knelt between my legs, I instructed him to just rub himself on me and to watch as he did it and that when he felt ready, to guide himself in.

The good student that he is, he followed my instructions. I helped him again to find his way in, as this was not the time for searching around and losing momentum. Once in, he began to move and with some guidance from me, moved in different directions, to get more sensation. He alternated between biting his lip and smiling, but his erection held, perhaps helped a little by the sounds of response from me. Though I'm very much in teacher mode in these situations, my body has a mind and responses of it's own and prompts those occasional little moans.

We continued on and I could feel that his erection would wane a little and then come back, but essentially, it held.

"How're you doing, James?" I asked.

"I'm doing okay, but I'm not getting there. Should I do something else, or...?"

"Nope, you're doing just fine. Remember, it's not about getting there. It's about having fun on the way and after all, once you get there, the trip is over, at least for the time being. Aren't you enjoying this and having fun?"

"Well, yeah, but…."

"Nope, no buts. That's the point. Coming will come when it comes. I'm certainly enjoying myself, but actually I think we need to stop here. Can you handle that?"

"Yeah" he agreed, as he lowered his weight onto me. "I'm actually surprised that I made it this far without losing it again."

I wrapped my arms around him and hugged him." You did great James! See, all is not lost."

"No, it sure isn't, but I'm sorry I couldn't go all the way."

"No need to apologize to me, I would have been pretty surprised if you had. Too much going on mentally, and emotionally, I'm sure."

What I could have told him was that the gallop home to the great yahoo, hardly ever happens at this point. In fact, I can't remember if it 's *ever* happened, unless the client tends towards early ejaculation.

"It's pretty normal, James. Not to worry, okay? For now, better reach down and hold the condom while you move. Our alarm is probably ready to go off."

He did so, sitting up and removing the condom as I got up and headed for the bathroom. When I returned, he was sitting on the edge of the bed, shriveled condom in hand.

I sat down and put my arms around him. He responded with a hug of his own and a small kiss.

"Thanks, coach. I feel much better. It was really good that we didn't stop."

"Yep, you're definitely getting there. It's going to be alright, you know."

"Yeah, I believe you." He gave me another squeeze and got up.

"You can get rid of that in the bathroom James."

I watched his tush as he disappeared through the door. Very nice! I shut off the alarm before it could sound its 'time to quit' chirping.

I was dressed and stripping the sheets off the bed when he returned. We made a little small talk as he dressed and then I told him, "James, until our next session, when you masturbate, and please do, try using a softer touch and really focusing on the sensations for awhile, like I had you do in the beginning. It's important that you get used to the more subtle feelings. And use a lubricant, too. That's what I wanted you to remind me about."

"Okay, I will."

I went up to him and put my arms around his neck. His hands around my waist felt comfortable and relaxed. "So how do you feel, now?"

"I feel good, again, like maybe I'm going to be okay."

"I'm sure you are. It's just a matter of time and practice." Another small hug and kiss and we headed down to the front door. Afterward I would make my report call to Dr. Johnston.

CHAPTER 19
JAMES

In the next several meetings, James encountered some difficult moments with the lack of cooperation from his penis. He had been doing his homework and getting used to a more gentle form of stimulation, and moving back and forth between that and a more stimulating grip, was able to sustain his erection and move to orgasm. In our times together however, his erection would wane and not come back during intercourse. We were able to bring it back by stopping and doing other things, but so far, sustaining intercourse for any length of time had been eluding us.

James was game though. Although he felt very frustrated from time to time, we both felt he was making progress and he certainly had, in all other aspects of lovemaking. He was becoming more and more capable of taking charge and said he really enjoyed doing that.

As I wanted him to be a well-rounded lover, we also spent a fair amount of time with me running the show, giving pleasure and himsimply receiving.

We explored a lot using different textures for hand stimulation. His arousal level would come up and remain fairly constant, which indicated to me that while it could be partly a matter of sensation, it might be more about lack of eroticism during intercourse. I felt like I needed to know what kind of emotions he was having as we approached intercourse each time. It seemed to me that his thoughts and feelings were the main hindrance to his sensation. He was much more tentative toward intercourse than any other form of lovemaking.

Orgasms were not a problem in and of themselves. Although we never made them the goal, when we had played enough, James had no problem coming with oral or manual stimulation.

During one of our sessions, as we were lying in the afterglow, I asked him, "James, I'd like you to think for a minute about what your feelings are about intercourse. How you feel as we begin it, and then if you can, tell me."

He lay on his back, eyebrows knitted together and I watched his jaw working as he chewed on his lip. His eyes were half closed as he looked down his body at his feet.

"Let me see. It's hard to describe. I guess I feel okay at the beginning, but then I start to feel, I don't know, nervous? Scared? Weak maybe. Yeah, even if I've felt good before up to that point, once I'm in I start to feel worried I won't be able to do it, that I'm not going to be any good and you'll be disappointed, I guess."

I thought about that for a minute. "So how are we going to steer you away from that feeling? What if you weren't concerned about me, but just went for an orgasm? Just as an exercise, to just go ahead and fuck and drive for it without worrying about how I'm feeling or responding? You could use whatever visualization or fantasy that you use when you masturbate, that really gets you hot, or maybe just the idea that you're going to fuck my brains out, would do it.

What do you think of that?" I was on my side facing him and he turned to face me as well, resting on his elbow.

"I don't know if I can do that. What about you? That feels kind of rough. Wouldn't you feel like I was using you, or something?"

"Well, let's just look at this as an exercise. You need to have an emotional reference point for a feeling of passion. We can always pull back, but you have to go there first. Both of us know that this is an exercise and I also know that you're not an uncaring or inconsiderate man. To add to that, I'm a strong woman, and can take care of myself, so I'm not afraid of being used. The trick here is for you to give yourself permission to do it."

"Right now, I can't imagine it," James said, with a little shrug. "I don't know what that would be like or feel like."

"Well, what I'd like you to do *is* imagine it. When you're masturbating, to imagine that you're fucking and you're going for it. Make a fantasy out of it and let yourself really get into it, if you can. Imagine even that it drives the woman wild, which by the way, is a good possibility. I myself love that wild male sometimes."

"You do? Hunh, I'd of thought you'd just like it kind of slow and sexy and all."

"Assumptions, my man," I laughed. "Sure, I do love that, but sometimes I like to be pinned down and taken….all in good fun, of course. Mostly, I like to feel my partner's passion. That's exciting! Sooo, are you game?"

We needed to dig out a raw, primitive male part of him, one that could pick up his sword, metaphorically and literally, and wield it with a sense of strength and confidence. Once James had experienced it, hopefully he would be able to enjoy and accept it and I knew that I could hold the energy for it.

I remember my spiritual teacher saying, "Women, be careful of what you nurture in your men." In other words, too much nurturing of a more sensitive nature in your man, and you may encourage a man that's lost his maleness. So, I needed here, with James, to teach him a sense of gentle caring in relationship, but also, to help him find a sense of his own masculine power. I felt it was just waiting to be discovered and it was an exciting thought to me.

James smiled, and shrugged again, "Well, you're making it sound kinda like fun, so yeah, I'll give it a try. It's a little intimidating right now, but I'll work on it."

"Good enough. So maybe we'll practice next time. In the meantime do the fantasizing I talked to you about, please."

"Yeah, okay. I'll see what I can dream up. Maybe something about you." He leaned forward to kiss my shoulder, then my neck, then my lips.

After a few moments, what began as a soft sweet kiss, felt like it could be turning to something else; a definite interest in his assignment, maybe. As he put his arm around me and pulled me closer, I could sense his arousal building and could definitely feel it, pushing at my belly.

"Whoa, hold up there guy," I teased as I began to hold him off. "We can't start practicing now. We're too short of time".

"Are you sure?" He whispered into my neck.

"Yep, sorry!"

With that, James threw himself backward onto his back, with his arm at an angle over his head, "Oh, all right, that's fine! I just thought you'd appreciate my enthusiasm," he teased.

I laughed, and responded, "Oh, I do, really. But it'll still have to wait."

"Fine, I'll be good and go home and practice," he grumbled, sticking his lower lip out, to hide a smirk.

"Great! So, let's get dressed and I'll see you out."

I had some thinking of my own to do about how to approach our next session and wanted to run the idea past Dr. Johnston.

CHAPTER 20

MASCULINE FEMININE BALANCE

I f we have the time, it is important to me that my client conclude their therapy with not only an ability to be open and sensitive, but also to be able to assert their maleness, their manliness. When necessary, to be able to pick up that symbolic sword I mentioned previously and use it, with decisiveness, confidence and passion. Depending on the client, one area or the other may need special attention.

One might be exhibiting masculine energies to such a degree that he is unable to empathize, speak openly about his feelings, or achieve any real degree of intimacy. In other words, with little yin or feminine sense of connectedness and I've had a good number of these in my practice.

Another might be so gentle that he becomes indecisive, tenuous and too soft in his approach; no yang or masculine assertive energy. More balanced, but inexperienced clients will often approach more tentatively, trying to be too careful, and need to be loosened up and learn how to have fun with their masculine self.

I do get the opportunity in our general work together to evaluate some areas that I see might have a correlation to a client's particular difficulty. An example I can give is that of a man in his early forties, I'll call him Joe, with long-standing, stubborn erectile problems. He was married in an open marriage with his wife and both of them had other lovers. Her other relationship had been going on for some time, and she was happy with it, but he was frustrated that he was having sexual problems with his serial lovers whom he generally met at sexuality workshops. His wife knew about and encouraged his working with a surrogate partner.

Clearly there's a great deal to say about the dynamics of his marriage, but what I would say here is that he and his wife experienced a great deal of physical intimacy, cuddling and talking honestly, with sweet pet names for one another. Unfortunately, not much going on in the actual intercourse department and the situation was the same with him and his other lovers.

Joe was very soft spoken, sensitive, and delicate and he had no problem expressing his feelings of pain, frustration and sadness. He felt comfortable in the area of touch, and was extremely gentle and caring, so much so, that it was obvious that he wasn't aware of his own sensations, but instead, more interested in making it good for me, so we needed to work a lot with sensate focus.

In addition, I also began to pay attention to his walk and noticed that he did so with smallish steps, shoulders slightly slumped, chin down, spine curved so that his butt tucked in and his pelvis and belly pushed forward.

Having done some instinctual work in body characterology (working with the expression of the body to affect emotional and psychological changes), I asked him if he would be willing to begin each session with me working on changing his walk.

I know that as one begins and continues to physically embody changes that may not be second nature or comfortable at first, new patterns are being established in the brain and new ways of thinking and feeling emerge. A more masculine way of walking in the world can result in a more masculine approach in relationship and in bed as well.

The client agreed enthusiastically, so we began each session practicing. As he walked back and forth in my living room, I made corrections for him. Longer, rolling strides, shoulders back, rib cage lifted up and over his belt, which brought his pelvis and butt back.

He reported that it was a very odd sensation, but after a couple of sessions and his practice outside our sessions, he said that walking that way seemed to give him sense of confidence and he had begun to feel more sexy. After awhile, he also began noticing that women were noticing him more, as well.

I based my work with Joe on the example of a pattern of body movement of a lover that I had when in my twenties. He was attractive enough but, more than that, when he walked down the street, he commanded attention. His strides were long and panther like and he walked with the air of confidence of a man who knew he not only exuded sex, but knew how to use his body.

He was a *very* manly man and it was true that he definitely knew what he was doing in bed. He certainly could have used a little more sensitivity and openness to communication, but in the physical sex department, he had no problems.

But, getting back to the client; I didn't expect, or intend, that Joe would achieve that level, but in an effort to give him some masculine balance, it was a good model to keep in mind. As we were working with his outward appearance, in our intimate times together I began urging him to be more assertive, to take charge.

While he was good at giving gentle pleasuring (paradoxically his own way of being in control), the idea of moving into an obvious, masculine show of assertion was not comfortable for him. I would have him move my body from one place to another, one position to another, without asking permission, to do things to me that he wanted to do, anything that was not harmful or painful, was okay and a playful little slap on the butt, now and then added a little spice.

It took some time, but as we played together, another side of him began to out itself, a side that liked being a little tough and dirty and his confidence in his ability to be assertive began to blossom.

However, when it was his turn to receive pleasure, he became very anxious about surrendering control. He needed to constantly control what was happening to him: a touch here, don't touch there, sort of thing, but we were making some progress with that and some success with his erections.

He also reported more success with his serial lover, and it felt to both of us that we were doing some very good work, when his own work schedule shifted. As a result of his changed circumstances, we had to conclude our sessions before we were entirely sure that his growth and changes had become more permanent.

I have heard from him a couple of times to learn that he and his wife had separated and he was with another woman, whom he reported, had a lusty appetite. There were still some problems, but on the whole things appeared to be better, so it seems that some of it stuck.

I see a lack of assertiveness, in varying degrees, in many clients. For Joe, his presentation in the world and his assertiveness in bed went hand in hand. Confidence and feeling attractive out there helps create confidence in the bedroom as well. Some other clients, like James, simply need to be able to give themselves permission to act on their desires.

I've given Joe as an extreme example to show the effect of what the lack of masculine energy in men can have and the importance of balance.

Other clients that might be heavily invested in the masculine, are often uncomfortable with intimacy, trust and openness. They can benefit from work with a more gentle focus in giving and receiving, in order to create whole, balanced relationships.

As for James, his issues with masculinity were not such that he required the same kind of work as Joe. James just needed to let that aspect of himself come out to play, unhindered by any sense of appropriateness or doing things just so.

CHAPTER 21
JAMES

My report to Dr. Johnston after my last session with James, had included my thoughts about how I felt James was holding back his passion and trying too hard to be careful and doing it right during intercourse. Dr Johnston felt it was a good insight and supported my idea of getting James to just go for it. The thing to determine was what approach would be the best.

After thinking about it for a while, I decided that a wild, somewhat debauched approach might work to overcome James over-thought approach to intercourse. While that could certainly be fun, I didn't want it to be intimidating and the big question for me was, could I do that as a planned thing?

Planning something that ordinarily tends to happen when my partner and I are highly aroused meant that I would have to let my teacher, therapist self go and let my own naughty or raw self be fully present. In this case, it might need to be role-playing, which could work, but didn't feel authentic to me. Finally, I decided we would just concentrate on arousal and see what unfolded in the moment.

I reminded myself that it didn't have to happen that day and that it probably wouldn't. Teaching James to feel his way to orgasm, rather than thinking his way to one, was probably going to be a step-by-step creatively repeated process.

When James arrived, we talked for a while about his budding relationship with Jennifer. They had been seeing each other for a few weeks and were getting along really well. She seemed to have a patient outlook on the idea of greater intimacy, but the closer she and James got to what looked like imminent sex, the more anxious James got. I understood his reluctance to talk to her about it, but urged him to at least think of how he might approach it. The worst scenario would be for Jen to interpret his failure to initiate sex as a lack of interest on his part.

I myself had personal experience with this kind of situation. In one relationship I had a partner who was unable to maintain his erection during intercourse in the beginning. We were able to talk about it however, discussing his frustration and mine with the s`ituation.

I was working as a professional surrogate at the time, but didn't want to have to act as a surrogate in my own relationship, so I decided to just be as understanding as possible and wait to see if time and lack of stress would improve the situation.

During that time there were a number of very frustrating evenings, for both of us, but mostly for him. We did everything else that brought us pleasure but intercourse evaded us and it became a point of pain in our intimate times together. As we talked and talked about our feelings and as he really trusted that I didn't judge him, things began to improve. Finally, after two months or so, he became able to sustain his erections and after that there was no problem, except for an occasional time, as with most men, when they're tired or stressed or really just not in the mood.

I figured that if Jennifer and James were to have sex and if she, in particular, could stick with it, eventually a lack of erections would not be a problem, as he became more comfortable. However, since James had the benefit of surrogate therapy, there was no reason for him to go through all that anxiety and frustration. If we were successful, and I was confident that we would be, our work together could prevent that.

This particular session our talk centered around the possibility of really letting go into sensation and feelings during our time together, allowing ourselves to act instinctually. I didn't want to set it up too much, or action on his part might stem from thinking about it and not from genuine feelings of high arousal. Some kind of push was definitely needed to help him overcome his anxiety about having intercourse with Jennifer.

James had gotten to be pretty comfortable with taking the lead during our preliminary flirtations, necking on the couch and initiating the more sexy stuff, so after we finished talking, it was only a short time before we were up stairs and in the bedroom, kissing and undressing each other.

I pushed him onto the bed and threw myself on him and we fooled around with who's mastering who. I teased him, avoiding his kisses when he was on top and devouring him when he was on the bottom, and both of us were getting hot.

His erection was in full bloom so sitting on top of his lower legs, I told him he had to lay absolutely still and I grabbed a condom from the side table, opened it, set it on the tip of his cock and performed my trick, holding it with my mouth and then pushing it down with my mouth and hands. Much sexier than letting him do it and didn't interrupt the moment.

Then I gave him my best oral sex, moving his hands back to his sides when he put them on my head. The idea was to drive him to the point where he couldn't think about anything else but coming. I brought him again and again to the place where I could hear his breath become deep and forceful and then I pulled back, slowing or stopping or changing movements, so he wouldn't come. I wanted him to save that so that when we had intercourse he could only go for it.

Each time I stopped, James would twist in frustration and reach for me, but again, I'd move his hands aside. No touch-ee, no feel-ee, absence makes the dick grow harder! I did this for quite awhile, keeping him at a peak arousal for an extended period.

Finally, I threw myself to the side, twisting around so that I faced him, my legs open. "Come on sweetie, come and get me, if you want it."

"Oh yeah." Jaw set, he wasted no time getting between my legs and positioning himself for the plunge and with a look of determination, he did. I folded him in to my body and grabbed his butt, encouraging him without words.

After a few hardy thrusts, James pulled back, looked at me and said, "Are you okay, is this okay?"

"Yes! Don't worry about me. I'm great! I'll tell you if I'm not. Just go baby, just fuck me!"

Given the permission he needed, he went for it and it couldn't have been more that two minutes before he shuddered and gasped, then groaned and came! *Yahoo!* I almost couldn't believe it.

I hadn't been sure it would happen with our first try, so I was a both little relieved and very happy for him when we were successful. Being able to reach orgasm during intercourse should go a long way in giving James some confidence.

There would be more work to do in upcoming sessions, of course, involving more of the same drive. In addition to that however, he needed to learn how to sustain his arousal while slowing down, in order to maintain for a while.

"Wow!... Wow!" James lifted himself off me, looking slightly stunned himself. "Man, that was great! You know, I wasn't even thinking about it, it just... happened, just like that. It was really fast though, too fast, but it caught me by surprise." His face looked as though he was afraid of my affirmation.

"James, that was more than just alright, it was really the point, this time, so just stay with the pleasure. You earned it." He lowered himself to rest again on my body and we lay quietly together, content. I could feel his strong heartbeat against my chest as it slowed in relaxation. Finally, James lifted again and we untangled ourselves to allow me curl up to him, my head on his shoulder. His hand stroked the arm I threw across his chest.

"I guess you didn't come too, right? James asked, sounding a little chagrined, as if he were at fault.

"No" I laughed, "I didn't, but that wasn't important for the moment. There'll be time for that later. I just want you to let your self go. Feel the passion and get used to it, enjoy it for a bit. Then you can learn to control it more."

"Yeah, I'm all for that." James grinned, and then his face took on that look that had begun to show itself more, when he felt confident…..the hidden lover was becoming not so hidden.

"So, what time is it?" He twisted to look at the clock. "Hey, whaddya know, we have a little time left. Maybe just enough time to make you a happy lady." He showed me his best lecherous eyebrow. "I'll do my best, anyway." He lifted and rolled over toward me.

That sounded delightful to me, and that eyebrow made me laugh as he got me into position. Then he got busy with hands and mouth and with a little help from self-stimulation on my part, in the twenty minutes we had left, he managed to make me quite happy. Satisfied indeed - with both of us, and our progress.

It seemed to me a breakthrough session and I was aware that although we still had some more work to do, the end of our working relationship loomed, not too far out there. James was a good client, motivated, willing (My favorite word; it gets so much done) and wanting to get on with the life he so desired.

We cleaned up the room and dressed and headed downstairs. James gave me a happy smile as I saw him out and I knew that Dr. Johnston's face would have the same smile, when I told him of our session. I couldn't help smiling myself.

CHAPTER 22

VIRGINS AND THE LAST, BEST STAGE

In the case of what I will call late life virgins, a range I would say is from the late twenties into the forties and fifties and beyond, there are so many levels to work through. First we deal with just being able to handle the closeness of another person and the emotions that arise from that. Then we add the sensate or sensual feeling, learning to focus on the body, usually something that has been denied out of shame, embarrassment or fear.

We keep adding on physical, dating and social skills, intimate communication, learning how to share feelings and literally, how to have sex. Having sex sounds like it should be simple, but to someone who has never done it, it's a very big and confusing deal.

All along the way, we are facing issues that were put in place in childhood, through family dynamics and often in strict religious upbringing. Once we have worked through all this, we reach a place where the client feels comfortable enough to begin meeting women, often through dating services, and personal ads.

If he's reached a point where he is getting out and socializing, he may meet someone on those occasions, but I find that to be unusual. Services and ads are a convenient way to find people that may be compatible and are the least threatening to new daters. Also, a first meeting over coffee is a non-committal way to make first contact and makes for an easy get away if it's not working out.

The dating period may take awhile and there may be a few awkward attempts at relationships. When one has been a loner most of one's life, it takes some time to learn to share with another person. Sometimes, in the process a client may get their heart bruised a little, but that's all part of the learning process; being able to recover, to see what part they played in the demise of the relationship and what they would like to do differently. Even learning how to remove one's self from a non-compatible relationship can be difficult. These are all issues that most people have dealt with in high school and college.

If the client and I are able to work together long enough, he may now have reached a stage where we can go to a new and deeper level of healing. This is the place of the heart. It's the place where the client really begins to trust his sexual nature, which has been hidden and suppressed for so long. Here he may be able to surrender to that aspect of himself and eventually express it.

At this stage, he will be able to be more open and vulnerable with a partner and able to make deeply intimate, delicious, sexy connections. Sex can become richer, more meaningful and definitely hotter and more fun.

This is always the place I prefer to reach with my clients, although it doesn't always work out. This is when I know they will be able to create and sustain relationships of substance. They will become teachers themselves through those relationships. They will be wonderful lovers and partners. This is what I love, this healing of the sexual, loving being.

It isn't often that I'm able to work with a client long enough to get to this point. Some clients are lucky enough to have the benefit of finances that allow it and some, having the innate sense that there is more to it all than just sex, do whatever is needed to be able to continue for a while.

For some clients though, just being able to function sexually is the greatest thing that could possibly happen at the time and those I send off with a kiss and a prayer for their continued growth and happiness out there in the world.

For myself, the stage of deepening with a client is the gravy, the real goodies of the work, I suppose because it provides me with a reflection of myself as a sexual, sensual being. When the client and I are relating at this level, I am free to express that part of my nature and this final chapter is fun, enlivening and very dear, for both of us. We linger here just long enough to establish a real confidence in the client and then it is time to terminate our work and say goodbye. At this stage, on my part, there is a deep sense of satisfaction, joy and indeed, some sadness.

I haven't always known what happens to clients over the years. The work is not a magic bullet, but it does offer new possibilities, a chance to have the kind of personal, intimate, sensual life most human beings want.

Some that come to get coping tools for a physiological dysfunction go after and achieve their goals and go back into the dating world to do very well, while others, though equipped with new skills and tools, are not emotionally prepared to do the things required to obtain what they want from life.

Clients that perhaps have been married for years and find themselves divorced and terrified of dating and unsure sexually, are usually quite successful in fairly short periods of time and able to enter the singles world and develop relationships.

I content myself with the knowledge that for some clients, just being held and nurtured is the most important thing they can experience and can open them to possibilities of simple friendships in their life.

There are many degrees of wounding and damage out there and while surrogate therapy doesn't guarantee any certain outcomes, it offers a chance for an intimate life. Well worth the investment of time and money, which is something that any successful client would say, I'm sure.

I have had a very few clients that were unable to work through a problem and terminated early, but these have been rare and I have given a few examples later in the book. Most people do come to understand that the issue that is arising, halting or impeding their progress in the moment is the reason that they need to be here in the first place and that it is coming forward to be dealt with and healed.

Unfortunately, knowing that doesn't prevent the feelings of frustration, sadness and shame that need to be weathered through in the process.

CHAPTER 23
JAMES

Although we'd made a huge step forward, James still had some physically trying times. Quickies were the most successful, but in our time together, James and I progressed from the idea of passionate quickies to the more extended arousal times. We didn't want to linger in the "come and get me" phase too long, as it was important to not imbed quick ejaculation as a way of life, sexually.

While he wasn't successful every time, I felt that he was beginning to be confident that his arousal would be there more often than not, and he began to be less frustrated when he was unable to maintain. We talked about the fact that he had spent a good portion of his adult life worrying about it and that his fear probably wouldn't go away like magic after one or two successful experiences.

When he couldn't sustain his erection, it gave him practice in how to deal with that situation as well. He learned to change it around and do more for me, converting the potentially ego-bruising experience to one in which he could take charge, give pleasure and increase the possibility for his own arousal again. He also became more assertive in asking for what he would like.

James had needed his own permission to really experience passion, to fully immerse him self in it, and once he started to grow comfortable with that, we began to move back into a slower kind of love-making. This of course, was also a very fearful place for him, because he felt that without the heightened drive of the quickie mind-set, he would lose his erection.

What he actually found after a short period of time, was that moving slowly didn't mean lack of passion. It was simply a controlled burn as opposed to a raging brush fire.

We also worked with hand stimulation, focusing on a one to ten scale, one being slightly interested, and ten being orgasm. The idea was for him to learn to gauge his pleasure level so that he could enjoy it and go with it (around six or seven), and not worry about shooting past enjoyment to an imminent orgasm, which would be eight (uh oh), to nine (Too late!) and then quickly to ten (Oh My God!!).

As he learned to ride the wave of six and seven with hand stimulation, telling me what changes to make or to slow down or speed up, he would be able to do the same thing himself during intercourse. He also had homework to practice this himself until he could maintain for at least fifteen minutes and ultimately to come when he wanted. This was all backup because, at this point anyway, early ejaculation was not really a problem, which would have required a much greater focus on this exercise.

During this time he and Jennifer were seeing each other often and had progressed in their relationship and were having what sounded like, some very promising, hot intimate times together that did not include intercourse.

James, surprisingly, *had* talked with Jen about the fact that he was seeing a therapist to deal with some problems sexually that had stemmed from some earlier situations and needed to proceed slowly. He did not say that it was surrogate therapy however, which was understandable.

Either Jennifer liked him so much that she felt him worth the wait, which I certainly thought true, or she was simply quite an amazing young woman, but in any case she had said that she felt okay with that and was willing to go slowly. They had begun having oral sex only, and while *she* seemed good with that stage, James, anxious, but hungry, wanted more, of course.

It might seem odd to some that James would want to talk to me about it first, rather than just going ahead and trying. He certainly didn't need my permission, but he did want some assurance, from me, and himself as well, that he was ready. I could only tell him that I felt he was, but there was no guarantee I could give him. There was never going to be the one perfect time, but I did feel that he now had the tools to deal with a problem, if one should arise. He had grown tremendously in that regard, and I asked him if he didn't think so too.

"Yeah, actually I do," he answered. "I know I'm not the same guy that came here back in May. I wouldn't even have met Jen, if I was, let alone be having sex with her, so yeah! I worry though, that she'll get impatient or tired of me."

The new, improved James, reclined back on the couch. He looked good, had lost a few pounds he said, visiting the gym more frequently. He generally had a more relaxed, even happy air about him, but at the moment his teeth chewing his lower lip showed his concern.

"Know what James? I think you know what you're doing, so why don't you just take a chance. So what if it doesn't go just as you might like the first few times. I think a woman who likes you would understand that and with experience and the comfort of familiarity, it'll get better. You've been very honest with her about your desire to take things slowly, and it seems that Jen does really like you. If she didn't, she wouldn't keep going out with you and you'd never even have made it to the oral sex stage. She's been patient so far you know, so it seems like you're the only one worried here. You don't need me to tell you what to do...you know very well, what to do. I think you should just go and let yourself go with her. Have fun. If the first time doesn't make the grade for you, well do it again! There's more where that came from. And that's what I have to say! There, that's my sort of tough love speech."

He nodded. "You're right. I'm just being a wimp. So, then what?" He turned and looked me, his brown eyes focusing intently on my blue. What happens with us, our work together?"

"Well, we'll see how it goes." I reached out to rub his arm, which felt strong and solid beneath his shirt. "I want to be here for support or any more coaching you might need, but once you feel relatively comfortable with it all, we'll have reached your goal and it will be time for you to go it on your own. How does that feel?"

"Sort of sad, I guess." He took his eyes from mine and looked down at his hands that seemed at the moment to be comforting each other with touch.

"Well, we knew there would be an end to this, right? But it's not quite here yet, so although we don't want to ignore it, we need to be ready, but we also need to keep moving ahead. Is the fact that we might be ending at some point soon, holding you back?"

His brows came together in a frown. "What do you mean?"

"I mean, I'd like you to think about it. Is it just the old fear of intercourse stopping you, or could it be what I said? That it would ultimately mean the end of our work together? It's just something to consider, you know."

"You mean not fucking Jen because that means you and I'll be over? Nah... No. At least I don't think so." He paused, thinking it over, his teeth working on his lower lip again.

"I don't know, maybe it's possible. It's really easy here with you. You make me feel okay with everything and when things don't go right, you're okay with it. I don't have to worry and I know you'll help me figure it out."

I nodded. "Well, it's good we're talking about it. Sometimes these not so obvious fears are tricky and they do a great job of sabotaging us. I know that *you* know the kinds of things you can do if the situation isn't working. You've done it here, on your own, without my prompting. You just need to take the leap and trust." I gave his hand a reassuring squeeze.

"Yeah, I know you're right. And I really do think she'd be all right with it. God knows, she's been patient so far. Maybe I've been waiting for the right moment, when it seems like I'm hard enough that it'll stay."

"James, as I said, there will never be the perfect time. You just have to do it. As far as you and I are concerned, it's going to be over, sooner or later, one way or another, and you know that. We can't go on forever and you deserve to have someone in your *own* life out there. I don't want you to let any fear of letting go of this situation keep you from living your life. If I thought you couldn't overcome that, I'd say maybe we should terminate right now, and let you go it on your own."

James shook his head. "No, we don't need to do that, because I want your help and feedback, for at least the first time or two. I can do it, really. I just didn't realize this separation thing" -he waved his hand between us – "might be a problem. I'm ready to give it a try! I sure want to." His smile reassured me, to say the least.

"Great, I'm glad." I smiled and leaned against him playfully. He put an arm around me and gave me a squeeze, laughing.

I was pretty sure that it was only a matter of a short time before we would have the conversation about ending our relationship, but I was looking forward to hearing of James' successes.

CHAPTER 24

MATTERS OF ATTRACTION, & CLIENTS THAT LEFT PREMATURELY

A question that clients never ask me, but one that other people do, is "what if you're not attracted to the client or they're not attracted to you?" I think for the client, in the beginning, it's a loaded question.

In their minds, that would open the door to honest discussion about their feelings about me, or mine about them, and it would be too risky to say or hear what's real. In truth, it might be that neither of us would be a person that the other would be attracted to, out in the world. The wonderful aspect of this work is that the process itself fosters sensual attraction and an ability to be present with and for each other, regardless of our preferences that make for personal attraction under normal circumstances.

For me, there is never a question, in terms of attraction, as to whether or not I can or will work with a client, but for myself, in the beginning, I usually try to find something about that person that I find attractive. It can be anything, like their eyes or the way their mouth works when they speak or even something in their personality, This usually happens in the first part of the first session, and quiets that young and critical part of myself that might want to say "yes, okay, it's good, I feel an attraction" or "nope, it's not happening."

Since I trust the work itself to do it's magic, it's only a temporary focus. However, it can take a bit longer for a client to overcome their preconceived ideas of who or what attracts them. Their sense of comfort with me is what allows them to let the work provide the sensual connection.

One client who stands out for me, in terms of attraction, was a quite obese man I'll call Roger. Although heavy, he was also very classy and dressed beautifully, something which, in that first meeting, I definitely found attractive. He was a man of the world, cultured, intelligent and creative, but the best thing about him for me was that he was a wordsmith. I'm very auditory; music, sounds, words all stimulate a great response in me. He used words in the most delicious way and he also found me beautiful and sexy, or so he said.

He had the erectile difficulties that some obese men have. Extreme weight and for some men, diabetes as well, affects vascular function, restricting blood flow to the penis, so strong erections might be hard to achieve and sustaining them when they do present, even harder. With Roger, cock rings worn at the base of the penis were very helpful, trapping the blood flow in the penis to keep it firm. That trick combined with sustained arousal periods of play and interaction brought him to the point that he felt that he could work with it himself. Viagra would probably have worked for him, but he chose not to use it at the time.

It was one of my shorter-term cases, and it was fun and very sweet. Before he left he wrote a couple of poems to me, about me, which, on days when I'm feeling insecure, I can pull out and read. When I do, I see myself through his eyes. What a gift! Extreme weight is an issue for me, but imagine if I had been put off by his weight, we would have missed all those yummy moments of words and sensation and pleasure.

I have only had a few clients in all my years of working that felt they didn't want to or couldn't work with me. One was a client younger than myself, maybe 15 years or so, and certainly not the youngest I've ever had, that couldn't handle the difference between the texture of my skin and a much younger woman's, although he had never been with anyone else at all. I just looked different, he said.

It's never easy to hear, whether the client stays or not, and if they leave without establishing a working relationship with me, I have to work with the part of me that recognizes that I've been rejected. Unfortunately, the case therapist involved was not at all helpful in pursuing the issue with the client and he left.

The solution for me in a case like this, is to understand that they were here in the first place because they had problems with intimate relationship to begin with, or perhaps, in his case, he might have had unconscious issues about his mother and the thought of being with someone older is too repugnant.

Others can only feel good about themselves based on who they are with, who is attracted to them. If it's someone they consider beautiful it reflects on their own sense of personal attractiveness.

For some, the whole idea of their sexuality is so frightening, that they have to sabotage their chances for healing. Whatever the issue, there is also sadness for me, because I know that if a client stays, our chances of overcoming the difficulty are extremely good. In fact, I've had a few clients, in the course of our work, change their feelings about not being attracted to me in the beginning, to the point that they later find me lovely to touch and very attractive.

One client, in his late forties, and generally attracted to women of college age, told me several times, that in the beginning he wasn't sure he could handle intimacy with me, but now loved my body.

Another client that left therapy with me was the only one that also left me with feelings of anger. He was from another country, one that culturally does not much consider the feelings of women. He came into surrogacy with erectile difficulties, for an intensive week of treatment and didn't say much about any feelings about me in the beginning.

In an intensive we work three hours a day, so by the third day we are getting deeper into intimacy, and he was definitely showing signs of arousal. All of a sudden that day, he announced that he wasn't turned on by me, wanted a younger surrogate, of which, at that time, there were few and not much younger at that. Even more, he wanted me to recommend one: this, from a man around my own age. It seemed to me that he couldn't deal with the fact that he *was* attracted to someone slightly older than himself and had to do with his own self-image.

He wouldn't hear any discussion of staying, so I called the therapist, who scheduled a therapy meeting with the three of us, the only one I've ever had to do for a crisis. Issues of money came up, and he refused to pay, but after much talk with the therapist, finally agreed to pay a portion of what he had contracted for. In addition, his manner of speaking about me was unkind, with harsh words. The whole thing was very disheartening. I was not sad to see him go and it took me some time to get over my feelings of anger toward him.

A second client, unfortunately from the same country, didn't even get past the second 2 hour session. He was not as harsh as the first one, but between the two of them, it left the therapist and me with the feeling that we didn't want to work with anyone again from any country that was so culturally disinclined toward women.

We both realized, of course that there are definitely exceptions to the rule, so it was possible we could reconsider under the right circumstances.

One of the clients I've had that left the work prematurely, did not leave because of a non- attraction issue. He came into therapy with erection problems and an inability to create a relationship for himself, even though he put himself into many situations where there were available women. He was in his mid forties and had been married with no children, but the marriage fell apart and the only information the therapist and I had was from his point of view and that was that she was "bad" and took advantage of him.

When I first met him I thought he looked kind of interesting; a big guy, nice enough looking, but a little rough around the edges. Despite that rough looking exterior, he was actually intelligent, fairly cultured, very well off financially and emotionally extremely sensitive.

He hadn't been able to establish a relationship since the end of his marriage and hadn't been successful sexually in his encounters. He had taken sexuality workshops and self-help seminars and had been doing things he enjoyed to potentially meet women. He had some uncomfortable, but minor, physical problems that no one could seem to correct and hated medical doctors, feeling that they had worsened them. He had a problem with depression and although he was on medication, would come to sessions in mental distress and it would take a good deal of processing to get to the intimate physical work.

As we spent time together talking, he would share his stories of grievances against women, often women in authority, but men were not omitted from his anger. In his eyes, he had been abandoned, misjudged, treated unfairly and accused. Many groups that he became involved in resulted in what he described as emotional injury to himself, either by the facilitator or some person or persons in the group.

His depression was extreme and he was dramatic in his self-deprecation. He worked with a primary therapist as well as the sex therapist and spoke sometimes of committing suicide if he didn't have a relationship by the time he was fifty. People say a lot of things when they're depressed, but some really mean it and with him I wasn't sure. His plan was several years off however, so we could only concentrate on the present moment and work with him to achieve his goals.

On his good days, we had some success physically. Quite comfortable with his body, he loved the touching and intimacy. We were able to share some laughter and light moments and were making progress with his erections and with our intimacy. I felt that he had begun to develop some trust and confidence in me and we were having some productive times together.

I tried to coach him on his interactions with women, although he would usually be drawn to women with whom there would probably be little chance of reciprocation. They were usually much younger, lived in another state or were already in a relationship.

When he was attracted to a woman and he thought she seemed more or less agreeable, he would come on strong, doing too much, trying to merge too quickly and invariably he would be rejected, which added to his anger and depression.

We would discuss the sessions he had with both his primary therapist and the sex therapist. When we had been working together for a several months or so, he came one day to our session in a dark and angry mood. He was furious with our sex therapist, who was trying to help him see the "glass as half-full," rather than "half empty." The therapist rapidly became one of the bad people, who had caused him injury by not honoring his feelings. The situation escalated and nothing that I, or the therapist could say or do, would soften his resentment and his primary therapist was of no help.

Although I had actually done nothing to injure him in this case, and we had been having an intimate, caring, surrogate relationship, I suddenly became "tainted," in his words, by my association with the therapist. He never expressed any anger directly toward me, but his libido in our sessions declined.

He finally demanded another sex therapist and with the agreement of our original therapist, I gave him a referral to another that I knew. He saw him for a short while, but finally told me that he couldn't get over my "taintedness," no matter how close we had been in the past, and terminated our work together as well as with the new therapist.

It was a very tough, anxiety-ridden time for both me, and the therapist. I myself had feelings of dismay, anger and confusion to deal with. I had been very supportive and loving and intimate with the client and all of a sudden, I had become unclean, in his eyes.

Thanks to my own personal psychological work, I was savvy enough, underneath the feelings, to know that it was really not my problem, nor the therapist's, but the client's own illness, and I was able to separate myself from those feelings after the break.

Neither the therapist nor I ever heard of him again, but I do think about him from time to time and hope that he was able to get the kind of help he needed and that his plan for suicide on his fiftieth birthday never came to fruition. I'd like to think that he was eventually able to find love.

One of the most difficult cases of my years of practice, I'm telling this story to show both sides of the work. While most clients fall into varying degrees of James' type of experience, once in awhile a more difficult case comes along that requires every bit of the psychological and emotional maturity I have attained in my practice and my life.

But when we receive a client that is really ready to do the work, willing to look at themselves, willing to change, wanting to move forward and do whatever it takes to do so, we have success.

A different kind of story of early client termination was Paul, a client in his mid to late forties, who had divorced about a year and a half earlier from his wife of 23 years. I gathered that it had not been an easy divorce, but because of his three children he maintained a respectful relationship with his ex-wife and saw his children often.

He was referred to me by a sex therapist for anxiety around the idea of dating and engaging sexually. He

Cheryl King

had married young and had never strayed outside of the relationship and felt that his experience was very limited. Just the idea of dating a new woman and having to interact in a more personal way, put him into a frozen state, unable to act.

A nice looking guy, to my mind, he had dark hair, dark eyes and a comfortably attractive body. He had his own small contracting business and dressed casually, generally in levi's and a shirt. I liked him. He was sweetly shy, but did his best to be open and honest with me.

He told me that he hadn't wanted the divorce and hadn't really understood why his wife did. She said that she simply didn't love him anymore, hadn't for a long time and wanted out to find someone else, which she subsequently did, shortly before he began seeing me. Because it was so soon after their divorce, he suspected, but didn't really know for sure, that she might have been seeing or known her new husband while she and Paul were married.

All of it left him feeling inadequate and his anger at her also turned inward on himself for not seeing it and for not being enough himself to make her happy. Now here he was, a man approaching fifty, with little experience with women, deserted and on his own.

Not the direction in which he had ever imagined his life moving.

When we began working with sensate caresses, he enjoyed my touching him, but when it came time to touch me he would break out in a sweat and his palms would be damp enough to require lots of baby powder. His touch felt tentative and I needed to remind him often to breath and relax. We had to work slowly and had trouble progressing, often staying at one level for several sessions. He was able to express his discomfort, although he couldn't explain it.

He had certainly touched his wife without such anxiety, but according to him, their sexual activity had declined to almost nothing in the last few years of their marriage. I also gathered that they were not explorative by nature, meaning that they most probably did the same thing most of the time.

His sweating continued throughout our first several sessions, although he seemed to be getting comfortable with me and we were able to laugh and joke together and snuggle. Finally, we had worked our way through the basic sensate touch sessions with a resulting decrease in his anxiety and sweating.

We spent a lot of time on relaxation exercises with some success and had made it up to kissing, where the sweating returned, accompanied by an uncontrollable trembling. And the trembling didn't stop as we continued on to more erotic play, spending extra time at each level. Relaxation helped, but every time we began moving into intimacy, it was there.

Finally one hot afternoon, as we were laying on my green futon, cooled air from the ceiling fan wafting around us, he told me that he felt he had to stop seeing me. When I asked why he felt that way, he replied that he had begun having feelings for me and knew that it couldn't go anywhere.

I told him that I'd like to see if we could work it out, but he seemed adamant. He did agree however, to discuss it with the therapist before making a final decision.

A week later, the therapist called and regretfully informed me that Paul's decision was final and that she had been unable to change his mind. He didn't want a referral to another surrogate for the time being however, and agreed to do a closure session with me.

The closure session with all clients is crucial. It's a chance to recapitulate; to look at what's been gained and what still needs to be done, but also importantly to talk about our feelings at parting. It's a chance to say goodbye, with no loose ends or energy tendrils hanging out and sticking to either one of us. No wondering or wishing - a clean break.

Paul kept his appointment and we shared some bites of food and a glass of wine. In the course of our talk together, I approached again the issue of his sweating and trembling. He said that he just felt too nervous with the intimacy to begin with, but that the fact that he liked me so much made him afraid of doing things wrong or of not being good enough and the closer we became, the worse the nervousness got.

He also admitted his fear that he would fall in love with me, and knowing that our relationship would end, was afraid of being hurt.

I told him I had dealt with this before, maybe not to this extreme, but that I still felt that if we hung in there, we could get through it to a place where he might feel very differently. But, for him, it was all too new, too much at the time and he had made up his mind. Maybe later he'd try again.

Given his determination to walk away, I resigned myself and surrendered to it, although I knew that I would carry it with me for a bit and that I had my work to do in letting go of my feelings of failure. My clients often hold the mirror for me.

I did tell him that I felt sad, but also said that I felt sure he could work through it at some point. So, we talked about what he could do, like keeping up with his relaxation and breathing exercises, and keeping a journal of his feelings.

I urged him to check out personal ads or some of the dot-com dating services, when he was ready, to push the edges of his envelope, to keep moving ahead, so as not to get stuck again. Also, to look for things to do that he himself would enjoy doing; groups, classes or events where he would find people of like mind and perhaps he might meet someone that way.

It was a sweet and sad meeting for both of us, and when he left I breathed a heavy sigh as I closed the door.

My time with Paul became a great reminder to let go of my own expectations for a client. Although *I* might feel incomplete or unsuccessful with the end result, sometimes the smallest wins or accomplishments can change a client's outlook and interaction with the world.

A few months later I received an email from Paul. He thanked me for everything, excited to tell me that he had met a woman and was in relationship with her due, he felt, to the work that we had done together. I myself had considered it unsuccessful, because he couldn't bring himself to complete it, even though I had had no control over his feelings. To his mind however, it had been a win, enough to help him change his life.

A year or so later, in returning from a trip, I passed him in a line at the airport. I would not have acknowledged him, as a matter of professional confidentiality, as he was with a woman, but as I passed he called my name.

I turned and with a big smile and a hug, he introduced me to his lady as a friend. We exchanged simple pleasantries and I left them feeling proud of him for his openness and also proud of, and delighted in, the work that I do.

As one can see, there are definitely some very difficult moments in this work. Because the nature of this process is so intimate, those times can have a personal effect, the material for some hard personal work on my part but, I have to say here, that for me, the rewarding times of doing this work far, far outweigh those moments.

CHAPTER 25

JAMES' SUCCESS

A few days after our conversation, regarding his readiness for the next step with Jen, James called to cancel our next appointment. He had taken action on our talk and invited Jen to go away for a long weekend, which would include the day of our scheduled meeting.

Although I didn't say anything, I had a little bit of concern that he might be trying too hard to make it the perfect time and setting, but realized also that spending long hours together, just relaxing and having fun, could create the environment he needed to let himself go.

Anxious to hear how it went, I was excited when I received an email from him after his long weekend, simply saying, "Had a great time. Lots to talk about. See you next week."

When I opened the door to James for our next session, he greeted me with a smile and a little salute of his hand before he stepped through the door.

"Come on, I want to hear all about it, but let's sit down." I hugged him and then steered him toward the living room and the couch.

"Hear about what?" he teased, with a perplexed look at me.

"You know what!" I exclaimed giving him a little push and settling back on the couch. "I assume from your happy look, that things went well?"

"Yeah, we had a really great time. Some good dinners, walks on the beach, talked a lot. She's a really cool woman. She's interested in lots of different things, like archaeology, so she's great to talk to. She's interested in me too, asks lot of questions about my family, my work, what I think about things, you know, like that. And on top of that I think she's really pretty and sexy. I think I could like her a lot."

"Hmmm, sounds like maybe you've already got a good start on that," I observed.

He nodded thoughtfully, "Yeah, maybe so. We got to know each other pretty well this weekend and there wasn't much I didn't like. She sort of just goes with the flow, you know what I mean?"

"Yes, I think so. So far it sounds really good. You know, it often takes my clients more time to weed through the dating services to find someone that they feel compatible with, so you've been pretty lucky. And so, how about the rest? Did that go well?"

"Well we had a little glitch at the beginning. I was pretty nervous and it wasn't like we just got crazy hot and fell into bed. It was more like we sort of just took our clothes off and got in and lay together with my arm around her. We hadn't actually talked about it, but somehow it seemed like we both knew we would try intercourse this time. I think she knew I was nervous too, but kind of like you, she just put her hand on my chest and started touching me, then we started kissing. When it got really hot I did get inside her, but after a little bit, I started losing my hard on." He shook his head rather wonderingly.

"She was so cool, though, I felt sort of okay about it. I kept trying to stay with what I was doing with her and not thinking about it and we just messed around for a while. When I went down on her, she came and it finally got me so hot that I got inside and kept going until I came."

He shook his head again, this time in exasperation. "I just went with it and everything I know about slowing down went out the window, so it didn't last very long. It was way too fast, actually. I think I was afraid that if I didn't go for it, I'd lose it again. I was in my head too much."

"Well, yay! For the first time that's great! It sounds like it was almost perfect. You actually did what you needed to, to get out of your anxiety and back into sensation, so terrific! Good job! And the rest of the weekend? More sex?"

James smiled that sexy, smirky little smile that mostly turns up one corner of his mouth, and gave a little tilt of his head. "Yeah, it went really well. After that I felt more relaxed about it I think. There were a couple of times that I got into the head thing, but between the two of us, Jen and me both, I got past it and we had a lot of fun."

Jen sounded to me like someone that might have made a great surrogate partner. I believe that some people are born with a gift of sensuality and combining that with a natural inclination toward psychology and healing gives you the makings for a life in intimate service. Of course, not all that are born with these talents choose this path, or there would be a lot more surrogate partners out there. Anyway, James was a lucky man to have met someone like her...a definite jackpot.

"So what's the plan ahead my dear. It sounds like you're settling into this relationship a bit?"

He nodded with a pleased smile. "Yeah, she says she really likes being with me and I like being with her, but I don't want to rush anything. This is all new to me. I don't even know what I'm *like* in relationship. I've been alone a long time you know, and a weekend is really great, but I have no idea what it would be like to actually be with someone 24 hours a day, all the time."

"Well, has that subject come up? Commitment, I mean?" I asked.

"No, not really. I'm new at this and maybe it just seems like that's where it would naturally go, but I'm not sure I'm ready for it. I like her a lot, but I don't really even know what she thinks about it. She hasn't brought it up and neither have I."

He looked a little sheepish as he confessed, "Actually I have a coffee date with a woman on Friday after work. I'm not sure why I made the date. Just checking things out, I guess. I haven't dated a lot and, oh hell, I don't know, maybe the whole thing makes me nervous."

I wasn't surprised that he felt that way, though more so that he realized that it might be because of a fear of commitment. Clients new to dating and re- lationship often find all kinds of reasons not to fully engage. "She talks too much," or, "She asks too many questions," or she's this or that or whatever and often, while some complaints are legitimate, under it all is plain old fear.

"Well it's good that you're observing that in your- self, and you know, there's no hurry. As you and Jen spend more time together, getting to know each other in all kinds of situations, your feelings will become clearer. The best thing to do would be to stay in the moment, not rush it and not project ahead. Just like we've always been doing here."

"Good reminder. Thanks coach, it helps to talk about it. What do you think about the coffee date?"

"You mean, do I think you should go? Well, more importantly, what do you think?" I took a sip of my water as I waited for his response.

"Well I guess it can't hurt and I feel like right now I need to keep my options open for awhile." He looked at me questioningly, possibly seeking reassurance.

"Sure, that's understandable. I think you'll know when and if you want to settle down with one person. But, on that topic, let me ask you a question." James nodded and sat forward and fastened his eyes on me.

"How are you feeling about our work together at this point?" I asked.

James hadn't confided any conflicting feelings about Jen or things he didn't like about her to me, and apart from his upcoming coffee date he had mostly stopped going on any first dates from the dating services, so it seemed as though, for the moment, he might be working toward a real relationship, despite the options thing. I like our work to overlap with a clients dating and being sexual, but if they're approaching a possible more committed relationship it's more than time to talk about termination.

"What do you mean? I think we've done really well together."

"I mean how do you feel about being with me at this point when you're beginning to have feelings for Jen?"

"You mean, do I feel like I'm cheating on her or something?"

"Well, I just want to be clear and because I'm feeling that we're getting close to finishing, I'm looking at our options."

"No, I don't feel like I'm cheating. You're my therapist and teacher, so it's a whole different thing, even though I like you and like being with you."

He settled back and threw one arm on the back of the couch and smiled. "But, I am feeling pretty good about where I am in the sex department, even though right now I've only had sex with two women in my whole life. I could probably still have problems if I was with someone else besides Jen, but I think I know what to do. The thing is, another woman might not be as cool as Jen about it."

"Yes, that's true, but that's something lots of men face, every time they're with someone new, and you have the tools to deal with it, as you've proven. You have a very sexy, sensual side to you James, you just need to let it out more and more. Play with it, what can it hurt?" I patted his thigh and gave it a squeeze.

The hand he placed on my own thigh, felt warm as he stroked it, "Well, maybe I'd want to play with it now," he hinted broadly.

Oh, there it was again, that sexy grin. I was such a sucker for it!

"Well, I don't know, maybe I need some convincing," I said, giving him a look over one shoulder.

His hand on the back of my neck pulled me in for a kiss. "I think I might be able to do that," he murmured to my lips. And after awhile on the couch, kissing, touching and getting some clothes off, I felt pretty convinced, so we went upstairs to give ourselves more room.

If James could allow himself to be as confident with other women, as he was with me, he would have little trouble. It was obvious that he felt more confident and good about himself as he did things he knew I liked, talking sweet dirty talk, and taking charge of my body.

As we moved together he said all the right things, like how beautiful and hot I was (something I think we women all love to hear) and accompanied that with all the various sounds humans can make when they're experiencing pleasure.

As we lay together afterward, his arm wrapped around me, I said "That was wonderful, James. That's the guy a woman wants to take her to bed. You just need to remember that he's in there."

"Yeah, I'm getting to know that part of myself a little bit and I like it. It sure feels better than before."

He was quiet a moment. "As a matter of fact, maybe we *should* talk about what you said earlier."

Knowing what was coming, I rose up on one elbow, to look at him.

"Finishing our work?"

"Yeah. Are you getting ready to throw me out?" He looked uncomfortable, so I reached out and put my hand on the side of his face.

"I'm not throwing you out. I know it's a little scary, but I do think you're ready. I was sort of waiting for you to get over the hump with Jen, to have a successful experience with someone else, and I feel that now we've accomplished the main goals that brought you to Dr. Johnston and me. I'd guess that's how you're feeling, too?"

The creamy blanket covering us in our comfy nest, slipped down to his waist as he sat up. As he looked down and fondled the satin edge of it, his face softened in thought.

"Well, I've sure come a long way. I mean having Jen in my life is more than I ever thought I'd have, before I started working with you, but I don't know, do you really think I'm ready to totally go out on my own?"

"Well, you have a relationship, which is more than lots of people, and you're both enjoying it sexually. It's new of course and you may not know where it's going, but that's the nature of, and part of, the fun of a new relationship. It's all about discovery and new experiences." I stroked his back softly, reassuringly.

"And yes, I do think you're ready to be on your own. You're doing really well and you'll just figure things out as you go along like everybody else." I looked up at him calmly, waiting for his response to this.

"His thoughtful face looked down at me, brown eyes intent, maybe a little sad. "You know, it scares me. Like being out there without a safety net, but I guess that has to happen sometime." He went quiet again, then continued after a minute. "Yeah, it feels like the right thing."

I sat up and he wrapped both arms around me and squeezed tightly. "But, I'd really miss you."

"I'll miss you too." I squeezed back. "But it's about time for the training wheels to come off, my friend."

"So what happens, next? How does this work? This wouldn't be the last time would it? That doesn't feel good."

I could feel his concern. "No, I have to talk to Dr. Johnston to see what he thinks. I know you have a session with him tomorrow and I'll call him today to discuss it with him, so the two of you can talk about it. If he agrees, then you and I will have a closure session. You'll need to stay with him for a while though, to keep you on track." I smiled and gave him a light kiss on the cheek, then went on.

"If he does agree then our next session will be our closure. It's an opportunity for us to talk about what you need to concentrate on in the future and a chance to say how we feel about what we've done together and how we feel about each other, and to say goodbye. I like to have a feast, where each of us brings something to eat or drink and we have a naked picnic. No sex, though."

"Aw, no fun and games?" He shrugged. "Just kidding. That would feel pretty weird anyway, to jump up out of bed and leave, for good." I didn't bother to say that it happens all the time to lots of people out in the world.

"So if he agrees, we'll have our last session next time," James mused. "Wow, suddenly it feels awfully soon! But, I do agree that it's time."

I nodded my assent. "Well, good. It sounds like we're on track, then. I'll speak with him again after your session with him and we can connect by phone or email, to make sure we're all on the same page. That way, if we're going to have closure, we can talk about what you want to bring for our picnic." With that, I gave him a quick, but hearty kiss and we rose to dress for what could be the next to last time.

After James left, I called Dr. Johnston and told him what we were thinking. He agreed that he felt that James was ready, but he would call me back after their session, when he would have a chance to discuss it with James.

The morning after their session he called and said that James was good with the decision and so was he. The end was now officially in sight.

CHAPTER 26

JAMES CLOSURE SESSION

The final session of my training included a naked food feast, where we spread a blanket on the floor and ate yummy finger foods, sometimes feeding each other things like bananas or strawberries, each person trying to out do the others with their provocative eating habits. Great fun, it became a model for me for my own closure sessions, and out of that, it began to be important for me to symbolically "break bread" together, before my client and I separated.

Although I always like to do the little farewell feast, particularly with longer-term clients, it doesn't always work out to do so. When it does, the client, the length of time we've worked together and the length of the session we have for closure (some are only one hour, some two) dictate whether we do it clothed or unclothed, but we always have finger food and something to drink. The closure feast is only possible because I work in my home, with access to a kitchen and not in an office.

The final session is an opportunity to express our feelings about the ending of our relationship, to look at and acknowledge the progress that's been made as well as to determine what areas still need focus and practice. Work on those remaining issues can be done in relationships in their own world. It's also a mixture of fond sadness, satisfaction with what's been done and gratitude for what we've shared.

When James arrived, the scent of coconut shrimp baking in the oven wafted out to greet him.

"Wow, something smells really good in here. Besides you, I mean!" He reached out and pulled me to him for a hug and a small kiss, holding me with one hand, a bottle of Chardonnay with the other.

As he stepped back, he held up the bottle. "What shall I do with this? I just got it from the cooler at the store so it's already cold."

"Great!" I took it out of his hand and set it on the table. "Let's just keep it here for now."

He reached into an inside pocket of his jacket and pulled out an envelope and a small box and handed them to me, then took off the coat and draped it on the back of a dining room chair.

I looked at the card and package in my hand "What's this? Is this for me?"

"Yeah. I just wanted to give you something. Is that okay?"

"Of course, it's wonderful, but let's save it for later, if you don't mind. I have a little something for you as well." I always love to give my clients some sort of little talisman that they can take home, to remind them of what they've accomplished. Whether we've been totally successful or not, only the most stubborn and resistant person would not have been changed to some degree. But, whatever their degree of success, I like to give them a tangible emblem of their growth.

Some of my clients also want to do something special, a card or some small gift, and some just express their thanks verbally. After spending so much time together and coming to know one another so intimately, it feels good, I think, to leave that person with something of yourself.

"James, why don't you open the wine while I get our feast together" I suggested, as we went into the kitchen. I dug out a corkscrew and gave it to him, then pulled the coconut shrimp out of the oven while he brought the wine to the kitchen and began his task. The warm, exotic aroma of coconut enveloped us as I took them off the baking sheet and placed them on a waiting plate.

"Shall I take this into the living room?" James asked.

"No, you know what? I'd like to do this upstairs." Smiling at him I said, "You can just take it up there."

I had already prepared the bed like a picnic, with a bright yellow cloth, and a few extra pillows scattered about for comfort.

He grinned back and took the open wine bottle and two glasses sitting on the counter and left the kitchen, disappearing into the small dining room and in a moment I could hear him climbing the stairs from the entryway to the second floor.

He reappeared at the kitchen door a minute later, still grinning. "It looks like fun up there! Can I help with something else?"

"Sure, you could take the shrimp up and put the plate on the bed and I'll be up in a minute," I responded.

He took the plate and disappeared again into the upper planes of the house.

I put the sauce for the shrimp and a few other noshes that I had already prepared on a tray and followed him with it a minute later, along with his card and gift. In a few short minutes, minus clothing, we were lying on the picnic bed, our bodies at right angles, heads fairly close. A lovely little array of goodies lay on the tray between us: hummus, fruits, cheese spread and crackers, and a few stuffed grape leaves, just for the sake of decadence.

James poured us each some wine and we raised our glasses in a toast. "To both of us for the work we've done together and to you James, may you have a bright future, filled with love, sex and fun." We clicked glasses and the crystal chimed festively.

For a few minutes we just munched and chatted about how good everything tasted, fed each other some bites of shrimp and strawberry and of course, the banana. We weren't nearly as messy or suggestive as the meal in my training. Our own feeding had a more sweet and only slightly seductive air about it. I must say though, he did spend quite some time on his strawberry, with a gleam in his eye and I may have spent just a little extra time on the banana.

Finally, when the food appreciation had slowed down a bit, I asked, "So, how are you feeling about all this, James?'

"You mean the picnic? It's fun! No, actually I know what you mean." He paused a moment, licking strawberry juice off his fingers. "Well, it's kind of mixed. One side of me is really excited about where I am and I'm sort of anxious to just get going and see what's going to happen next. I like Jen a lot." His soft expression confirmed this and I smiled to myself. What a long way he'd come.

"She's great and I'm excited to see if it might work out for us, so that's all good. The last coffee date I had with that other woman didn't really mean anything. She talked too much and we didn't connect at all. It made me really appreciate Jen though, so I think I'll just hang with her and see what happens."

I gave him a big, delighted smile. This is exactly where I love a client to be before we terminate our work, and I felt so happy and grateful that we had the time together to overlap with the beginnings of what could be a real relationship for him.

His smile dimmed a bit as he continued. "On the other hand, another part of me is really kind of sad. I've always known this time would come and I felt like I had it in perspective, but now that it's here, I realize that I'm really going to miss you. I'll miss our talks and jokes and as close as we've been. It sure wasn't easy all the time, but you've been so patient and you've helped me so much."

He paused, looking at me directly. "I guess I've come to think of you as a really good friend, that I could talk to about anything, and I'm going to miss that. A lot!" He looked down and herded a few crumbs together on the yellow tablecloth. From where I sat to his side, his brown eyes looked a little too bright.

I sighed. "Yeah, me too. I'm going to miss you as well James. You've been so willing to go into physical and emotional places you've never been, that it's made it pretty easy to help you and I've come to think of you as a friend too. I've had some great laughs and some very sweet moments with you and on top of that, you always did your homework! I love that!"

We both laughed. How many times had I told him how great that was?

"And, I feel sad too. There's a spot every week that has been James' and now you won't be there, and I'm already feeling that empty space." I reached across the corner of the cloth and placed my hand on his cheek, turning his face to look directly at me.

"But, I am also so pleased and happy for you, sweetie. You've done so well and now, if this new relationship with Jen does go forward, it's up to you to create all those things that you'll miss here, in it, with her."

He sighed and rolled from his side onto his back, "Yeah, I know. Honest talk, being a good listener, sharing myself. I remember, and if it feels as good with her as I've felt it here, I can do it."

"Well, if it goes into a long term relationship, it'll be better than here, because I assume that you'll both be in love, right? I cocked my head at him and raised my eyebrows.

He laughed. "Yeah, I guess. If I even know what that is. Never been there." His head down, he looked sideways at me, and said teasingly, "I've sure been in lust though."

His face said "with you," and made me laugh again. "Um-hm, definitely some lust, and also, you and I've been caring for each other, I think, but caring is not *in love*. That's a whole different ball game and you'll know when it happens for real. Just trust yourself James. You have all the tools."

He nodded and I reached out and put my hand on his chest. "You've become a good lover you know, and you'll only get better with time. You may have mishaps along the way, who doesn't? But don't allow yourself to shut down. You know that your body works just fine when you're relaxed and just enjoying yourself, so try not to get frustrated when something isn't working. Just move into doing something else you both enjoy or talk about it with your partner. Remember that the goal in sex is about pleasure, not orgasm and you know that there are many ways to please a woman and yourself besides intercourse."

"Yeah, I know, and I think I've got a pretty good handle on that. What do you think? I mean the pleasing a woman part?"

I smiled. "Well, you certainly have it down as far as I'm concerned, but I'm able to tell you what I want. I know you've said that Jen has some problem with that, like a lot of women do. But you have to just keep encouraging her and telling her that you like it when she asks."

"Yeah, and I do like it when I get past the part that says I'm supposed to know how to do everything," James responded.

"Well, the thing is, a woman may have had a bit of sex, but it may not all have been good, or even satisfactory and they haven't known how to speak up or ask for what they need and want, so you can be a teacher here. After all, you've been to school in sex and relationship. You studied hard and now you're graduating with honors." I looked into his eyes, letting him know I truly believed it.

"Yeah. In a way it's all hard to believe. There was a point, before I started with you, when I thought it would never be possible, and now…man! Here I am with a girl-friend. I think, anyway. We'll see how it goes, but I like her and we're havin' sex!" He smiled a happy, "pleased with himself" smile and sat up, retrieving his glass of wine from the end table and taking a sip.

James looked different to me now. Some of it was familiarity, but he also had achieved a certain ease in his manner that was quite attractive and the anxiousness I had seen in him when he first came to me, was no longer as apparent. Maybe some of what I now saw was because he was comfortable with me, but I really felt that mainly he had come to be more comfortable with himself.

The crumbs of our feast, scattered across the little plates on the yellow picnic cloth between our bodies, were just in the way at this point.

"Why don't we move this off onto the floor so we can hang together for a little bit," I suggested, folding over the edges of the cloth closest to me to contain the debris.

"Yeah, I want to give you your present and I'd rather do that without anything between us." He got up and moved the tray onto the nightstand and stacked the little plates, so that I could gather the cloth into a ball, trapping any escapee crumbs. We set everything on the floor at the foot of the bed and crawled back up and fluffed the pillows, so that we could lean back.

James reached over and picked up the gift and card from my altar table next to the bed, where I had placed them beside my small gift for him, wrapped in a red cloth and tied with sisal.

He handed it to me expectantly, smiling. "I hope you like it. I tried to find something that would really say how I feel about you and everything you've done for me. How much your help has meant to me."

"James, that's so sweet of you." I leaned over and gave him a strawberry kiss, which he responded to by cradling my face in his hand. It was a gentle, caring touch and felt very dear.

I opened the card first. The photo on the front was in black and white, probably from the fifties, of a small boy in a black cowboy hat, with one foot in the stirrup, hanging from the saddle of a very large horse.

Inside, James wrote, "Cheryl, somehow this card just seemed to fit the situation. A cowboy learning to ride a horse bigger than he ever imagined! Thank you for being my guide, mentor, lover and friend. Thank you for sharing your body with me. It's a precious gift and it's been an honor and a privilege. I promise to take what I've learned and use it well and to be the best lover I can possibly be and to always value myself and my partners and most of all, to do my best to love without fear."

Touched by the card and the honoring in it, I couldn't speak for a few moments. I just looked at him and I knew that my eyes spoke everything.

All I could say was "James…" and I touched his cheek softly.

A little awkward and shy all of a sudden, he pushed the little gift box toward me. "Open this, now."

I held the little white box for a moment, still feeling a fullness in my chest from his words, then opened it carefully. There appeared another smaller velvet box inside. I took the little jewelry box out and opened it, revealing a lovely small gold filigree heart and delicate chain.

"Oh James, this is beautiful. Gosh, I'm speechless, for once. Thank you so much!'

He beamed and put his arm around my shoulder. "You're welcome. You've given me hope for the future and I wanted to give you something to know how much that means to me."

"And it means so much to me that you're in such a good place. It means that we've done a really good job, the two of us. I love this and when I wear it or see it, I'll think of you."

I gave him a hug then said "Now, I have something for you, too. It's something that's meaningful to me and it's to remind you of the power of love and sexuality." I handed him the red package.

"Hey, I didn't expect this. Isn't the student supposed to give the teacher the apple? "

"Yes, but my spiritual teacher always gives gifts and every time I see them or hold them, I'm right there in that moment and I guess I want you to remember your moments of growth in the same way."

He carefully untied the sisal and opened the cloth to reveal a small bronze statue of Shiva and his consort, in a Tantric position, facing one another, she on his lap with her legs wrapped around him. We had actually tried this at one point, and it had been a deeply intimate moment, so it seemed a good reminder for him of the importance of real connection in sexuality.

"Hey, I remember this. Yeah! This is great! Thank you! I'll put it somewhere I can see it every day. It'll remind me of you and me and maybe I'll be able to make those kind of times happen for me and someone else...maybe even Jen." He cradled the little figurine in his palm, hefting it, as if testing its weight and meaning in his life now.

"Well, whether it's Jen or not, I know that you'll be able to find love, if that's what you want. You're ready to go and I'm proud of you and I have a lot of confidence in you. But now, our time is getting short, so is there anything else you want to say or ask, or anything?"

James' eyes wandered around the room as he thought about my question. They lingered here and there on different objects as if consigning them to memory. "You know, I don't think so. I feel good and pretty done. How about you? Any last words?"

"Nope, I feel pretty done myself. So maybe just one last naked hug and then I'm going to send you on your way. It's time."

We stood up and James put his arms around me and gave me a tight squeeze. "I'll miss you," he murmured. "And I'll never forget you."

I felt my heart clench and I heard the catch in my voice as I whispered "Me too, you." Then I let myself go into the warmth of the hug between us. We stood in a melancholy glow for a minute and then it was time to part and dress.

"Can I help you with all this?" James asked, waving at the remnants of our picnic in a heap on the floor. I smiled, recognizing the slight moment of awkwardness.

"No, I'll take care of it, but thanks. We need to get you going." I began to get dressed, knowing that he would do the same. Sometimes there's a tendency to linger, just because it's hard, even painful, to say goodbye, so at this point, I'm the one in charge of moving things toward our final conclusion.

We were quiet as we dressed, both feeling the weight of the moment. James was putting on his shoes and socks when I said "You remember I said we can't have contact for at least six months, but at the end of that time, if you want to email or call me, to let me know how you're doing, I'd really love that."

"Sure I will, and I hope the news will be all good. But it'll be great to talk to you again anyway. Six months seems like a really long time, but I understand the reason for it." He stood and took my hand. "Thanks again, for everything you've done for me Cheryl. It's been amazing."

I gave his hand a squeeze. "It has and you're so welcome. It's been a privilege and a pleasure. Now, come on, I'll see you to the door."

James picked up my gift to him and we made our way down the stairs to the entry and stood facing each other, a little awkwardly, before hugging one another again.

I had a quick flashback of him when he first appeared at my door, nervous and unsure: Quite a difference from the James now who stepped forward into his future with some confidence and self-assurance. Then I moved to the door, and held the screen open for him as he stepped out. He turned one last time. "Take care of yourself, Cheryl."

"I will James. And you do the same. I'll look forward to hearing good stuff from you in the future. Good luck."

I gave a small wave and he did the same, disappearing around the corner of the house and down the walk. When he was out of sight, I shut the door and leaned against it, giving myself a moment to indulge my feelings. Finally, as my emotions settled, I moved to the phone to leave my report with Dr Johnston. Done and well done! And I felt very good!

CHAPTER 27

INTENSIVES

When a person lives in an area in which there is no surrogate therapy offered, what we can offer is an intensive course of therapy, of one or two weeks, primarily in the area where a surrogate has their practice, or in some cases the surrogate may travel to the patient. In either case, there must be a therapist willing to be part of the triad.

In this process, the surrogate and client see each other for three hours a day and the client goes on to see the therapist for one hour and there is, of course, homework each night.

An intensive is aptly named, because the work is so concentrated that emotions and the original cause of the presenting problem can rise fairly quickly. When a person has been stuck in a particular way of thinking of or experiencing their body for a long time, being asked to challenge that can be draining, even when it's done in a safe and compassionate environment.

Though we see each other for three hours a day, we can only move forward as quickly as the client's comfort allows. Because we have limited time, the client might be anxious and want to move too quickly, unable to sense where he or she is emotionally or psychologically, so we might have to slow them down, in order to ground the work.

When clients come to an intensive saying things like "You're my last hope" or "I know you're going to fix me" or "I need you to fix me," I always tell them that the intensive is just the beginning. The real work begins when they re-enter their life, but they will return home with tools for change. A therapist I know likens it to learning to play golf. When you've never played before, you have to hit hundreds of balls to be good at it. Practice, practice, practice!

Sometimes a client might opt to come back at a later date for further work, but when one lives out of town, an intensive is an expensive process. Not only is there the surrogate partner's fee for three hours and the therapist's for an hour a day, there is the air travel, hotel and meals and that is the case whether the surrogate travels there or the client comes to them. Some clients that have had a good measure of success the first time around, feel that it is worth the expense, after a period of time to assimilate what they learned the first time, to come back to do further work.

The same qualities that make a successful client in weekly surrogate therapy, willingness, motivation and responsibility for their own wellbeing, make for a successful client in an intensive. In an even bigger way, that is what will carry them through on their own.

To address both sides of the issue, I have had some clients that, although they felt they had received good tools and information in the intensive, were unable to sustain their level of development in the world. These were mostly cases that had to do more with virgins in sexuality and relationship rather than actual physical dysfunction.

My feeling about that is that those clients were alone and had no support, and a lifetime of feeling broken takes more than one or two weeks to overcome. It's just the beginning.

I've come to feel strongly that after an intensive it is extremely helpful for the client to have a therapist of their own, or even a close friend, someone who knows that they have gone through this process and can support them in taking what they've learned into the world. I know that's not always possible, but that's my hope and wish for them.

Some intensives have been fairly dramatic, while others are a slow, almost minute progression toward healing. Some clients do not enter that healing space, at least not in a place and time to be seen by myself. One of my most painful memories is of the client that emailed me sometime after his return home saying "They say surrogate therapy is 90% effective, but I guess I'm just one of the other 10%." He thanked me for my help and directed his self-declared failure at himself. Though I know that the client is probably 85% responsible for their own healing, it is painful when I know they feel they have failed, but I can't hold their hand when they leave. I can give them the tools, but they must be motivated to use them to change their own life.

On the other hand, I'd like to relate the case of a man that was referred to me that actually had the support of his partner, which gave him the advantage of someone to work with when he returned home. What I believed at the time would have been and indeed could have been a success story, if not for financial restrictions.

Rick lived in the Midwest with his wife and baby and intimacy difficulties in their marriage came to the point where his wife actually did the research to find a surrogate.

What a wise, brave and pro-active woman! She wanted more from her husband and she wanted him to heal from his childhood wounding, so that he could be fully with her and she was willing to do whatever needed to be done, to get it.

When I spoke with him on the phone, his voice was warm, personable and almost matter of fact, as he spoke of his childhood.

From the time he was six years old to nine he had been sexually used by his day care provider. He did sexual things for her and he saw it as his job that he did every day. No one knew about it of course and an intimate bond developed between them and Rick said it was the most intimate he'd ever been with anyone. When he was taken away from day care to be cared for by his grandmother, his sense of abandonment and loneliness was extreme.

Bodies love to be touched, so there can be pleasure when something feels good, but when the touching is done as a dirty, shameful or bad secret, the child comes away from the experience feeling that about themselves, as Rick did. He hated his body, thought it was ugly and dirty and had extreme shame around feelings of pleasure and arousal. Eye contact was extremely difficult, as he feared that people would see how dirty he was, and also because that kind of intimacy meant abandonment as well.

By the time he came to me, he and his wife had been married ten years. During that time he told me, they had shared little eye contact and lying together meant that he spooned her, so that she couldn't really see him, and she had never seen him naked with the lights on. He was able to have sex, with certain kinds of stimulation, but always felt that it was for her, because he loved her and not for him so he shut off his own pleasure. Also, orgasm was a shameful thing and something to feel very bad about, which made it difficult to achieve. By doing certain things he was able to have them, at least enough to father one child.

The biggest thing in Rick's favor was his attitude, which was "I came here for this, to be healed, and even if it's hard, that's what I came for and I'm going to do whatever it takes."

Every step we took, looked to him as hard to do at the outset, but he would forge on using the mantra we came up with of, "I can easily do this." For a man who hadn't allowed himself to be touched much, once we began, he took to the sensate caresses and after a short while came to be able to relax somewhat.

We used the exercise that I always use with clients to get our clothes off the first time and undressed back to back, before we looked at each other.

The mirror work, looking at ourselves in the mirror and talking about our bodies, was a valuable tool, giving me information as to the level of shame and feelings of disgust he had about his body. It also however, became a tool for beginning to change those feelings. When he had finished his turn in front of the mirror, I asked him to see if he could find one thing about himself that he liked. After a minute of deliberation, he responded with, "I guess my arms. People tell me that they look good."

That was a beginning, even if it was based on other people's opinion. He said okay when I asked him if he would like to hear about what I saw as I watched him standing there, so I told him the truth, that what I saw was a strong and powerful man…with a heart.

He seemed to like that, so his homework was to look in the mirror every day and affirm that to himself, which he did, every morning after his shower. It would take time and lots of work but each step in this work can make a difference.

With each step he blossomed a little more, like a rose whose petals were opening one at a time.

At some point, the sensate caresses, as they became more intimate, began to be arousing for him, which was great, because it wasn't his regular road to arousal with the specific things that usually worked for him.

Eye contact continued to be an area of discomfort, but when reminded, he could do it, however uncomfortable it was. It was an old habitual fear that was present even in his everyday interactions.

Receiving pleasure and accepting that it was a natural and healthy response was the main issue, so we spent a lot of time touching. It felt out of control and helpless for him to receive touch and pleasure was forbidden, so much so, that he had difficulty recognizing that he was experiencing it even as his body was responding. The trick was for him to learn to accept real pleasure in both. Just lying together naked, facing each other and looking at one another while touching was a big step and one that he intended to continue with his wife when they were home.

We had five days or fifteen hours together and Rick made incredible progress, but we both knew that he would need more work and he intended to make another trip to do another five days, after he had had time to assimilate and practice what he had learned.

By the time we had finished with our five days, he definitely had learned that he was capable of experiencing the pleasure of arousal, but a lot more was needed to really ground it in his psychology and his body. Given his background, a key aspect of that grounding was to be able to change his mental and emotional framework around pleasure, to be able to accept that he deserved to have it and that it was natural and good. From there, true intimacy would be an ongoing exploration.

Intercourse was not a part of our work together.

Rick was a delight, full of hope and determination! What an adventure and a gift, to be along on this man's journey to realizing the beauty and power of his body, his eroticism and the rewards of deeper intimate connections freer of shame and fear.

Work with him continued with two more 3 hour sessions over a period of three months, which is definitely not a productive way to work, and he eventually had to terminate because he couldn't afford it. Expense is always an issue, particularly since surrogate therapy is not covered by insurance as some traditional therapy is.

What a tragedy, but given attitudes about sexuality in this country, not a surprise, that people in need of this kind of therapy must pay for it entirely themselves. The pain that results from sexual physical dysfunction or a disability in intimacy and love is as real as any physical or mental dis-ease. One is not able to lead one's life in the way human beings were intended.

While Intensive Surrogate Therapy almost always has some level of success, giving tools, knowledge and comfortability, it is at its most successful when a client has the resources and is highly motivated and determined, making it a profound and life changing event.

CHAPTER 28

WHY SURROGATE THERAPY

The Surrogate Therapy profession is fascinating, extremely valuable, and very much needed. In our society, as generally repressive and unhealthy in attitudes about sexuality as it is, (partly evidenced by the fact that it is not covered by insurance) not much is known about it, even among therapists. A sad state, considering all the lives that could be taking changed by seeing any intimate dysfunction as a condition that can be and deserves to be treated. In some other countries there are clinics that offer Surrogate Partner Therapy along with regular therapy.

Unless they are comfortable and knowledgeable in the sexual arena themselves, a therapist working with someone who has sexual problems, as well as their original presenting issues, can be frustrated or even confused as to what to do with their client.

In addition, their hands are ethically tied when it comes to any kind of intimate contact with that person. A sex therapist, one that has been extensively trained in sexual therapy, certainly knows how to instruct and guide the client, which is extremely helpful and often successful, but again their hands are tied.

Nothing substitutes for hands on experience. It carries information to and from the body that the brain cannot conceive on it's own and emotionally and psychologically, the underlying issues arise for healing when the body has a sensate experience.

Neuroscience now tells us that body experiences of doing something new begin to create new neural pathways in the brain, and from my standpoint that affords great possibilities for change.

Couples in sexual counseling have a good chance of making changes, because they can work together, but if one doesn't have a partner, whom do they practice with? How do they change without body knowledge or skills or confidence around all that? A surrogate offers tools, guidance, and the experiences required for confidence building, and the triad model adds acceleration to the clients' talk therapy.

I hope this book will be helpful in dispelling some of the myths about surrogate partner therapy. Sexual gratification is never the goal in this work. It is really about the whole person and their relationship with themselves and others. Even when the difficulty appears to be strictly mechanical there are generally related issues. While the correct mechanics can be taught, those issues need to be addressed and with the therapists help, that is just what we do.

One of my clients that graduated with honors told me in our closure session, that his girlfriend told him that she was sure that he had had many, many lovers, because he touched and made love like no man she had ever been with. He was having a hard time convincing her that there hadn't been that many. Actually, he had been a late life virgin when he came to me and in the course of our time together, had had very short sexual relationships with other women before her, only twice. I hope that this story will give some ideas to the reader.

My greatest wish for this endeavor is that it might give hope to someone, either male or female, who needs it for healing, because it is possible, and one's life can change in so many ways through this patient, compassionate, instructive and loving process.

Along with that is the wish that a therapist reading this might more fully understand the work and begin to consider referring clients, male or female, to surrogate partners.

IPSA, the International Surrogates Association (www.surrogatetherapy.org) and it's surrogate partners are networking to make themselves better known, giving presentations at conferences for Quad S, The Society for the Scientific Study of Sexuality and AASECT, the American Association of Sexuality Educators, Counselors and Therapists, to better inform therapists about our work.

Also, "The Sessions," a beautiful film starring Helen Hunt came out in 2012 about a disabled man's experience in the 80's with a Bay Area surrogate, Cheryl Cohen-Green. Well received and nominated for several Academy Awards, it gave a new understanding of surrogate partner therapy and stirred a good amount of interest in it.

I feel privileged to have been able to do this work. Surrogate therapy has been an on going teacher for me, prodding me into self-examination, time and time again, guiding me ever further toward emotional maturity and a sense of personal wholeness. To see the positive changes my clients have made in their lives, including their relationships, has given me great joy, satisfaction and a sense of fulfillment.

Surrogacy has defined me for a number of years, but at this point it is exciting to imagine what other self-definitions are in store for me in the future. Although I am doing some of my best work at the moment, I feel that my time in surrogacy will be drawing to a close in the next few years and it certainly is not without some sadness that I write these words.

To the exceptional women and men who do this work, please consider this book a toast to you, my fellow colleagues and healers! And to the future surrogate partners and the therapists that come forward to do this very important healing service, I applaud you and welcome you.

And for my brave amazing clients, thank you for giving me your hope and trust and for being my teachers as well. I have learned from you and received from each one of you, something of great value to my own personal work and my sense of self...and I keep memories of each of you.

In return I trust that I have served you well.

www.ingramcontent.com/pod-product-compliance
Lightning Source LLC
Chambersburg PA
CBHW022002090426
42741CB00007B/861